Sustaining a Free Society

Sustaining a Free Society

Roles and Responsibilities of Citizens, Leaders, and Schools

Roger Soder

ROWMAN & LITTLEFIELD
Lanham • Boulder • New York • London

Published by Rowman & Littlefield
An imprint of The Rowman & Littlefield Publishing Group, Inc.
4501 Forbes Boulevard, Suite 200, Lanham, Maryland 20706
www.rowman.com

6 Tinworth Street, London, SE11 5AL, United Kingdom

Copyright © 2021 by Roger Soder

All rights reserved. No part of this book may be reproduced in any form or by any electronic or mechanical means, including information storage and retrieval systems, without written permission from the publisher, except by a reviewer who may quote passages in a review.

British Library Cataloguing in Publication Information Available

Library of Congress Cataloging-in-Publication Data

Names: Soder, Roger, 1943– author.
Title: Sustaining a free society : roles and responsibilities of citizens, leaders, and schools / Roger Soder.
Description: Lanham, Maryland : Rowman & Littlefield, 2021. | Includes bibliographical references. | Summary: "The central contention of this book is that a free society can exist only if the conditions enabling that society are understood and acted on. If these conditions are not met, the free society cannot long exist, or will exist in name only"— Provided by publisher.
Identifiers: LCCN 2021021628 (print) | LCCN 2021021629 (ebook) | ISBN 9781475861259 (cloth) | ISBN 9781475861266 (paperback) | ISBN 9781475861273 (epub)
Subjects: LCSH: Democracy and education—United States. | Civics—Study and teaching—United States.
Classification: LCC LC89 .S64 2021 (print) | LCC LC89 (ebook) | DDC 370.11/5—dc23
LC record available at https://lccn.loc.gov/2021021628
LC ebook record available at https://lccn.loc.gov/2021021629

Contents

Preface	vii
Acknowledgments	ix
Introduction	xi
Chapter 1: Political and Cultural Conditions Necessary for a Free Society	1
Chapter 2: Long-Term Perspective in a Free Society	23
Chapter 3: Leadership in and for a Free Society	41
Chapter 4: Citizens in and for a Free Society	61
Chapter 5: Schools and the Sustaining of a Free Society	79
Chapter 6: The Free Society: Reflections and Directions	99
Bibliography	113
About the Author	123

Preface

To write about a free society might seem to be an effective way to attract a congenial and self-satisfied audience. After all, most of us are enthusiastic about living in a free society. We like what we see as the benefits. We like to be left alone. We like to be free to choose. And what we want for ourselves, we want for our children, their children, and all those who come after us in the pleasing hope that those generations to come will be well situated in their freedom to choose.

But after more than four decades of teaching and writing about a free society, I have found that the audience's congeniality and self-satisfaction diminish whenever I begin to speak about what it takes to have and sustain a free society and what it takes to bequeath a free society to those coming after.

A free society does indeed allow a good deal of freedom to choose. But a free society can only be sustained if we all recognize that there is one critical area in which there can be no real choice. The central contention of this book is that a free society can exist only if the conditions enabling that society are understood and acted on. If these conditions are not met, the free society cannot long exist, or will exist in name only.

Put another way, we are free to choose to ignore the requirements of a free society but only at the inevitable cost of losing that free society. We are, in a sense, free to ignore those costs and plow blithely ahead. But the demands of a free society are not to be mocked. If we do not attend to the proper care and feeding of a free society, we will lose it or it will abandon us. And if we do not know what it takes to have a free society and how to value it, we will have nothing to bequeath to those who come after.

As such, I have written this book not to renew self-satisfaction but to encourage a willingness to look at ourselves and our responsibilities. I am asking the reader to weigh and consider claims about the demanding nature of a free society.

This book uses language in a plain way. That plainness starts with the book's title: *Sustaining a Free Society*. It is taken as a given that a free society is a desired good. It is taken as a given that sustaining a free society is difficult. If sustaining were easy, no book would be necessary.

The book is intended for the general reader. It is not a philosophical treatise for academics. I am not trying to cover all of the literature on any given concept, but I do try to suggest here and there sources that are easily located to go to for further exploration.

The book was not written in response to recent political and cultural events. The elements of a free society are perennial, and the issues and tensions surrounding these elements have been with us for thousands of years. But all of what is here is practically applicable to our time and our political circumstances.

The concepts in the book serve as a template for assessing leaders—and ourselves. For example, one of the conditions necessary for a free society is to be a more thoughtful public rather than a persuaded audience. We may say we do indeed want to be a more thoughtful public and not just a herd of sheep bleating in agreement with a leader. We can then look at the characteristics of a more thoughtful public and ask our leaders—and ourselves—what we and those we have chosen to lead are doing to enhance those characteristics. Thus, we have a grounded basis for assessment, and we become more likely to eschew partisanship and ad hominem arguments.

The book is, in effect, a series of propositions to be considered. In this world, freedom is always better than oppression. Thoughtfulness is always better than demagoguery and lying. Civil discourse is always better than mob rule. Facts are always better than conspiracy theories. There are no conclusive demonstrative proofs, either philosophical or statistical, for the view of the world offered here. In the end, in this world, we have our views and we must have, let us hope, opportunities to talk with each other.

Acknowledgments

I owe thanks to many people who have in various ways helped me try to better understand and work with the world of a free society. In particular I give thanks to three friends and colleagues: Gene Edgar, Bill Mester, and Spencer Welch. Each in his own way has provided insights, gentle critiques, and much-needed support, all with patience and humor. Much of what emerges in this book is due to them.

I also give thanks to Ralph Lerner, someone I have for many years in my classes characterized as my all-time favorite teacher. It was clear to me, even back then in 1961, as a freshman in a Soc I class at the University of Chicago, that our teacher, Ralph Lerner, had a strong sense of the moral obligations of teaching, of what he expected of us, and what he expected of himself. He and I have stayed in touch over the ensuing six decades. He has always maintained and met high standards of scholarship, teaching, writing, and civility—standards that I have endeavored to meet. Above all, I have tried to act on his observation to me years ago: the only way to truly reward a teacher is with a generosity of spirit.

When I was first planning this manuscript, I turned for help as always to Paula McMannon, a good friend and colleague over some three decades. She was kind enough once again to agree to help out. With her unfailing skills, she has put the manuscript in good order and gently lessened errors and the awkward phrase. The book is much better for her careful work; remaining errors and awkwardness are my responsibility. In many respects, Paula has always seemed to me very like my dear sister, Lenita. Both are caring and kind; both truly understand and act on the moral obligation to pay attention to others and to the world around them.

To my wife, Jane, I owe thanks and more, not just for this book, but for making my life a wondrous delight over all the years we have been blessed to be together.

Introduction

The book consists of six chapters, each dealing with one or another aspect of a free society.

What is meant by a free society can be seen not by long definitions but by the fifteen necessary conditions outlined in chapter 1. The fifteen conditions, in effect, define the free society. It will be seen that the conditions encompass both political elements (for example, how laws are enacted) and cultural elements (for example, the reasons why we obey—or do not obey—the laws we have). Chapter 1 also includes a consideration of what people need to know about how to know the world, along with a discussion of the tension between doing the right thing for the right reasons and politics as the art of the possible.

In chapter 2, we consider more closely one of the necessary conditions: the need for a long-term time perspective and the dangers we face by limiting ourselves to the immediate. Discussed here are the disadvantages of the short term and the reasons why the short term continues to prevail, along with a consideration of what is involved in trying to shift our basic time perspective.

The role of leaders in securing and sustaining a free society is discussed in chapter 3. That role involves persuasion, and we consider both the ethics of how we choose to persuade others as well as the ecology of persuasion—that is, how our choices of argument influence how other people will choose to talk. Of particular concern is the relationship between leaders and those they would lead—the citizens of a free society—a relationship that asks leaders to be neither dictators nor lapdogs.

In chapter 4, the emphasis is reversed. We consider the responsibilities of citizens—their responsibilities for their own behavior as well as what they need to do to ensure that their chosen leaders are, in turn, fulfilling their responsibilities. Included here is a discussion of the need for grounded individual and social identity, as well as the need for tolerance for ambiguity; also discussed is the need for careful and active listening, as well as the need for a careful view toward our past as well as our future.

In chapter 5, we consider what it takes to help succeeding generations know and value a free society so that those generations can, in turn, do the same for those who will succeed them. Knowing and valuing are matters of learning. Although learning can surely take place in all sorts of societal agencies (for example, home, religious organizations, and community groups), schools and, in particular, public schools play the central part of learning about a free society. Considered here are the critical relationships of both citizens and leaders with the schools. Moreover, the chapter includes a discussion of basic factors and constraints of schools and schooling systems, as well as a consideration of basic necessary elements of civic education.

In chapter 6, we conclude the volume, not with a summary of what has gone before but a discussion of three critical factors. We discuss the importance of not just *having* a free society but *deserving* a free society. We consider the need for imagination, for envisioning the possible as well as the probable. Above all, we consider the need to go beyond a free society in acknowledging and acting on our moral obligation to pay attention to other people.

Beyond an outline of how the book is structured, it may be helpful to talk briefly about how structure and content might be approached. Woody Guthrie said he wanted to be remembered as someone who told you what you already knew. In terms of cognitive learning, his approach makes sense. Perhaps you, the reader, may not already know all of what I am trying to get at. But many times you will have your own general knowledge and experiences to draw on and will quickly see the common points, or you will see that what is being said is roughly the same as what you know, but with a slightly different perspective or viewpoint. A given concept won't seem so alien that you have no way to hook onto it and link to what you know. You read, you listen, you quickly recognize the pattern.

The disadvantage of rapid pattern recognition is that once we see the pattern and we place the concept being read about in that pattern, we consider our job done and stop asking further questions about the concept. As such, what I am saying about a given idea may be very close to your own thinking, so close that you think you understand and can move right on through to the next idea. But there are always false cognates, and perhaps it would be good not to be too rushed. There may be similarities, but it is the minor—or not so minor after all—differences that often matter. The plainness of the language and the brevity of the book should not encourage rapidity of reading, but quite the opposite.

Chapter 1

Political and Cultural Conditions Necessary for a Free Society

A free society, like any society, is necessarily a political society for at least two reasons. There are groups of people, not just one person, in a society. And any group of people must deal with the fact that there never are enough resources for all. The perennial issue is how to allocate scarce resources. Priorities have to be established. Claims have to be made. Justification must be offered—if only the justification of force and the interests of the stronger. In a free society, like any society the allocation of scarce resources is a fundamental question, the question encapsulated in the title of Harold Lasswell's book, *Politics: Who Gets What, When, How?*[1]

A free society is political, then, in the sense that it must have some institutions, some laws, some orderly procedures for allocation. Without political order, there would perhaps be the dismal sight of war of all against all. Perhaps in one's dreams of a utopia, political order would not be needed because everybody would be in tune with perfection. Reality, however, isn't a dream, and we have to agree with James Madison's observation that "if men were angels, no government would be necessary."[2]

So a free society has some order, it has laws. But there is always a related question to consider: why do we obey the laws enacted? And with this question—why do we behave the way we do?—we are on cultural ground. Consider, for example, a law limiting the number of clams that can be taken daily at an ocean beach. The law itself is political. But the law exists in relation to people, and people choose to obey or not obey the law. Why people choose what they do is a cultural matter, with choices stemming from the way people have been taught to behave. There will be variance in the teachings, of course, and variance in the responses to those teachings. Some people will obey the clam limit law because they don't want to get caught and have to pay a fine. Others will obey because they believe the law is the law, and all laws should be followed without question. Others will obey the law because they think it is wrong to take more than one's share, and going over the limit will mean other people will have less than their fair share. For these people, the law itself is secondary, something to be obeyed, but it is not a primary motivator of behavior.

The reasons for obeying laws are as important as the laws themselves. If in a given society the predominant reason for obeying the law is fear of punishment, then a sense of calculation will pervade relationships between people and their views of how the world works. There will be a general sense of fear. Beyond that, there will be a sense of craftiness, of calculation, of individual gain irrespective of others, a sense of do what you will as long as you don't get caught. And we will offer to others, explicitly and by example, our view of how the world works.

But if the predominant reason for obeying stems from a moral sense, a sense of nature's limits, of being careful of what you take because of the needs of others, now and in the future, then overall the society tends to be on normative ground. On these grounds, we do what we do, not because of the law, but because of how we believe we and other people should behave. There might well be calculation here, but it is calculation in terms of the good of ourselves in relation to other people as well as in relation to the good of larger society, rather than calculation of individual gain at the expense of others. Again, by our example and through explicit teaching, we will offer to others our view of how the world works.

We have all sorts of choices to be made, too, in multitudes of nonlegal, nonpolitical, situations. And all of these choices contribute to an understanding of how a given society works. Consider, for example, some of the behaviors that can be observed while riding on a city bus during morning rush hours. Let us first consider what might happen while riding on a crowded bus standing next to another standee. Suddenly the bus jerks to avoid something, the person next to you begins to fall. What happens next? Most of us, without giving it any thought, will reach out, help steady the person about to fall. And most of us behave this way, reaching out without giving it any thought; the reaction is practically automatic.

Now consider another crowded bus, nobody standing, but one in which there are no empty seats. The bus pulls to a stop, someone gets on, an elderly person tottering a bit. Some people sitting near the front of the bus will get up, offering their seat to the elderly person. Others will contrive not to notice the elderly person and will find their reading device demanding their full concentration. They notice, but they refuse to give up their seat. Still others won't have any choice to make in this situation, because they have noticed nothing at all and have no awareness of anybody other than themselves.

In looking at these bus behaviors, we can perhaps make some distinctions. In one way or another, the first example of behavior suggests that there are some things we do more or less automatically, without conscious choice. There most likely is little one can do to teach others (or ourselves) to change our choices. But the second example clearly suggests choices, and choices that can be learned about and possibly altered.

A free society, like any society, is a complex combination of the political and the cultural, of choices made about reasons for obeying or not obeying laws and, in many nonlegal but cultural instances, choices made about our relationships with others. We are, then, in the realm of what professor and student of political philosophy Ralph Lerner suggests goes to make a political regime actual—its "institutions, procedures, and habits of mind,"[3]—and we are in the realm of what Tocqueville suggested, "habits of the heart."[4]

Let us assume that we want a free society, for ourselves and for our posterity. Determining what it will take to secure and sustain a free society is no easy task. We have the complex web of institutions, procedures, habits of mind, and habits of the heart to consider. Our task can become somewhat more manageable, however, if we recognize that a free society does not exist in a vacuum, unconnected to the conditions in its environment. Conditions are enabling, they are the prerequisites, the necessary factors.

Identification of necessary conditions helps us focus, helps us get a sense of what needs to be in place in order for a desired objective to be achieved. Let us say that our objective is to get from Seattle to San Francisco in the evening, and it is now late morning. In order to achieve our goal, we have to ensure that a set of conditions is in place. There has to be a flight scheduled for some time in the afternoon or evening. We have to have a ticket for the flight. The weather has to be reasonable. There have to be no shutdowns at airports.

There are four ways to approach consideration of conditions. First, we consider a condition in its ideal sense. For example, we can look at "equal justice under law" as a necessary condition for a free society, as an ideal. In the best of all possible worlds, what can we say equal justice under law means? Second, having done that, we can view the condition in another sense: to what extent does the desired condition exist? Is equal justice under law a condition that is distributed equally throughout the society? Or are there some portions of society that enjoy equal justice under law while for other portions of the society the notion is an unrealized ideal?

A third way of viewing desired conditions concerns how we can best move from what we have to what we think we should have, what we think all should have. And a fourth way of viewing desired conditions is to consider what conditions have to be in place to help ensure that future generations will be able to have the desired conditions and will be able to work toward further improvement. Conditions, just like the free society itself, do not just sit there, frozen in amber, guaranteed to exist in a fully operating state forever.

WHAT, THEN, ARE THE NECESSARY CONDITIONS, THE ENABLING VARIABLES FOR A FREE SOCIETY?

Conditions for a Healthy Free Society

Following are fifteen conditions hypothesized as necessary for the existence of a healthy free society. The set of conditions covers considerable ground in terms of institutions, procedures, habits of mind, and habits of the heart. That said, the coverage is not comprehensive. Others will find that some of the hypothesized conditions are not relevant or that there are conditions that need to be added. Following the discussion of the fifteen conditions, we consider two additional perspectives that further inform our understanding of what is necessary for a free society.

TRUST

If there is no trust, people will not be able to enter into authentic long-term relationships necessary for political and social action.[5] Without trust, there will be a tendency to move toward a society of war of all against all—hardly conducive to the operation of a healthy free society. So trust must be encouraged. We can think of trust in terms of relationships among people. We have need to have trust in our institutions. Moreover, we need to have trust in "an established set of facts necessary for the operation of a democratic society."[6]

Trust is complex, and its complexities must be learned. As usual, moderation is the key. A general willingness to trust must be tempered by a prudent skepticism (as with, in discussions of disarmament, "trust, but verify"). We might think, too, of typical advice to children—don't trust strangers—and we are quite rightly concerned about "blind" trust.

An equally important question deals with the recovery of trust. It is reasonably certain that for most of us, in one way or another, trust will be violated. Trust relationships built up over a long period can be threatened and often destroyed in a few sad seconds. In like manner, trust in facts and institutions can be violated. What needs to be learned is how to recover and reconstitute trust relationships. Recovery is sometimes not possible. Even where possible, the process of recovery can take years, even generations.

SOCIAL CAPITAL

Social capital has been defined in many ways.[7] At a minimum, we can say that social capital involves close networks of people who engage in reciprocal relationships. In a neighborhood with social capital, people help each other out by exchanging favors. The favors can be modest. When one family has to go out of town, a neighbor takes care of that family's pets. Sometime later on, the family informally returns the favor by loaning out, say, needed tools to the neighbor. The relationship is informal and nonmonetary. The neighbor does not charge money for taking care of the pets, nor does the family charge money for loaning the tools. With the exchange of favors comes talk, and more talk, and more exchange, and more reinforcement of trust in each other. One trusts the other to take good care of the pets; the other trusts that tools will be cared for and returned in good condition.

Other neighbors may be involved as well, building—and building on—close social ties. Those in such neighborhoods can do more than exchange tools. They get together in small groups, in perhaps informal groups in the neighborhood, to talk about the need for a neighborhood watch program, or the need for more street lighting or a stoplight.

By contrast, in a neighborhood with little social capital, people do not know each other, they rarely talk with each other. If there are improvements needed in the neighborhood, the impetus will have come from outside—the city government and its several agencies—rather than from the neighborhood people themselves.

Social capital is important to a free society, with small groups of people having the energy and the social and political skills to work together to get things done. At the same time, care must be taken that somehow social capital is widely distributed. Creating and acting upon dense social networks take time and resources and thus are more likely to be seen in wealthy neighborhoods while poor neighborhoods are left out.[8]

RESPECT FOR EQUAL JUSTICE UNDER LAW

The notion of equal justice under law can be interpreted in many ways. For our working purposes here, we can say that justice and due process of law must be available to all in equal measure irrespective of one's wealth, social position, or political connections. As the old folk song has it, "if you're rich, you can buy and sell the law," but we must try to make sure the sentiments in the song are at least minimized.

If there is no justice, we have no recourse other than self-interest, which is ultimately self-defeating. We must encourage respect for the law, even when decisions go against perceived self-interest or what we think is just. We must encourage the rejection of temptations to take the law into our own hands: vengeance is not ours.

FREEDOM

There are many definitions of freedom. For our purposes here, freedom can be defined as Herbert Muller construed it in his *Issues of Freedom* as "the condition of being able to choose and carry out purposes."[9] Freedom thus involves the absence of external constraints, actual ability combined with actual means, and conscious choice. You have to have the power to exercise freedom as well as the insight to value it. Both conditions are necessary. If one does not value freedom, it will matter little if one has the capabilities to exercise it. For those without the power to use their freedom, freedom is at most a dream.

In his history of the Persian War, Herodotus gives us an early sense of what freedom means. A Persian satrap tries to convince the Greeks to surrender to his king. The Greeks reply that the satrap is a one-sided counselor: "A slave's life you understand, but never having tasted liberty, you do not know whether it be sweet or no. Had you known what freedom is, you would have bidden us fight for it."[10]

We can argue that freedom is an inherent part of the human condition, not something bestowed from on high. Not everyone agrees. There are those who in one way or another side with the Grand Inquisitor in Dostoevsky's *The Brothers Karamazov*. In a long monologue, perhaps the high point of the novel, the Grand Inquisitor (although not Dostoevsky) claims that people don't want freedom, that they find freedom a burden, that they want to shed that burden, and that he, the Grand Inquisitor, and a few of his colleagues accept the burden of freedom from the people. The people are "free" to make inconsequential choices as they pursue their limited range of happiness, and part of that happiness is to be ruled in effect by miracle, mystery, and authority.

The Grand Inquisitor's position on freedom is close to Oliver Cromwell's view of the people: "It is not what they want, but what is good for them—that is the question."[11] Similarly, in 1774, an advisor to the Empress Maria Theresa said that it was desirable that there be schools for the great mass of people in order "to create 'good citizens,' that is, faithful and obedient subjects of the authorities." Further, the advisor noted, "Happiness is possible for all classes of society as long as one is pure of heart, free of unhealthy desires, and content with one's station in life into which they were born."[12]

There will always be a struggle between those who do believe that freedom is an inherent part of the human condition and those who believe that most people either don't want freedom or are unable to handle freedom. We must encourage a willingness to consider—but to reject—the claims of those who want freedom for themselves and a few select others but would deny freedom for all.

RECOGNITION OF THE NECESSARY TENSION BETWEEN FREEDOM AND ORDER

Political philosopher Leo Strauss reminds us that we must deal with the "freedom that is not license and the order that is not oppression."[13] If we maximize freedom and ignore order, we end up with anarchy. But if in our desire for order we move beyond reasonable order, then we are no better off. We have to constantly distinguish, as George Washington reminds us, "between burthens proceeding from a disregard to their convenience and those resulting from inevitable exigencies of society."[14] We must encourage a willingness to accept and act on the enduring and necessary tension between the two goods of freedom and order. As with the need for *e pluribus unum*, we must encourage a willingness to understand and in fact encourage the tension rather than try to seek an either-or solution.

One might wonder why one condition specified is "freedom," and the one immediately following deals with the "necessary tension between freedom and order." The separation is intentional, stemming from many observations that when the tension between freedom and order becomes particularly acute, the tendency is to move much more to the side of order at the expense of freedom. In order to stress the need to fight against that inevitable tendency, "freedom" is first set out as a condition all of its own.

RECOGNITION OF THE NEED FOR *E* PLURIBUS UNUM

A free society must be experienced by all, not simply by a few in this or that isolated group. There must be some sort of glue that holds the whole together, while at the same time maintaining respect for individual and group differences. What is needed is to acknowledge and deal with the necessary tension between the *unum* and the *pluribus*. In our time, we seem to place considerable emphasis on the *pluribus*, resulting in possibly self-limiting politics of identity and group self-calculation.

PEOPLE ARE THE ULTIMATE GUARDIANS OF THEIR OWN LIBERTY

In descriptive and reflective comments on his efforts to secure legislation for schools, Jefferson considers that "of all the views of this law none is more important, none is more legitimate, than that of rendering the people the safe, as they are the ultimate, guardians of their own liberty."[15] Jefferson's formulation has been expanded slightly by Ralph Lerner.

In speaking of Benjamin Rush and his concern for schools that would develop good citizens, Lerner notes Rush's belief (and hope) that schools "would go far in inculcating the technical skills and moral lessons that might render the people safe and knowing guardians of their own liberty."[16] Both skills and morality are necessary. Those with technical skills but no moral grounding can be dangerous, effecting political havoc. Those with moral grounding but lacking the technical skills will be weak and ineffectual in the political arena.

Lerner also joins "safe" with "knowing," perhaps using "safe" as something more than just meaning "assured." To be a safe guardian, but without the knowledge of what you are guarding and of what is at stake, is to be a robot. But there can be unsafe ways of guarding. One thinks of armed guards, of widespread open carry situations, with self-appointed guardians looking for action.

The notion of both Jefferson and Lerner, however, ends in the same place. People must be guardians of their own liberty. It is dangerous, ultimately fatal, to rely on others—dictators or mercenaries—to guard their liberty. Here we can seek counsel in the old adage: never invite a wolf to protect you when dogs attack.

KNOWLEDGE OF RIGHTS

A free society can hardly be free if we don't know what our rights are. In a free society, we need to know our rights, we need to value our rights, we need to have the wherewithal to exercise our rights and defend against threats to our rights. We will have difficulty exercising them. In his first annual address to Congress, George Washington speaks of the need to teach "the people themselves to know and value their own rights; to discern and provide against invasions of them; to distinguish between oppression and the necessary exercise of lawful authority."[17] We must encourage a willingness to believe that human rights are essential and that rights are natural rather than positive. Our rights are not bestowed on us by this or that leader (and thus if bestowed, capable of being taken away if we displease that leader). Our rights are human rights, ours as part of what it means to be human.

We must, then, encourage a willingness for a people in a free society to be "alert, assertive, and mindful of its honor, interest, and happiness."[18] To that end, Lerner reminds us that "the language of rights is not that of supplication" and that "claimants must be mindful of that which is due them; governors must be reminded that they govern a people who know what is due them."[19]

SELF-INTEREST WELL UNDERSTOOD

During his visit to America, Tocqueville observed a good deal of what he termed "individualism," the headlong pursuit of one's own interests. That was a kind of radical individualism, in which no other interests are considered. But at the same time, Tocqueville noted distinctions being made. He devotes an entire chapter, plus references elsewhere, in *Democracy in America* to the notion of "How the Americans Combat Individualism by the Doctrine of Self-Interest Well Understood." The Americans, he suggested, have a good sense that "man, in serving those like him, serves himself, and that his particular interest is to do good." Americans "almost always know to combine their own well-being with that of their fellow-citizens." Their "enlightened love of themselves constantly brings them to aide each other and disposes them willingly to sacrifice a part of their time and their wealth to the good of the state."[20]

In our own time, we can see the distinction and the advantage of pursuit of self-interest well understood. When asked why she was supporting the school levy despite not having any children, a colleague replied, "I may not have kids, but I have to live with yours." This kind of self-interest brings together the private and the public spheres. Pursuit of radical individualism, maximizing on returns in the private sphere and having no interest in anything but itself, always threatens the well-being of the larger society through withholding of needed support. There are some school districts that have a minority of families with children in public school. In these districts, school levies would not pass if voters all maintained a radical individualism stance. It is only because of voters who, despite having no children of their own in school, recognize the importance of schooling for all—including themselves.

Self-interest well understood may not in itself be a kind of pure virtue, but the results are beneficial and virtuous in a modest and practical way. Societal agencies receive needed support, but beyond that, a combination of the private and public brings people out of their narrowly inward focus to a participation in public affairs through involvement with others, and thus people in some sense become citizens rather than economic isolates. It is in this sense, then, that self-interest well understood is a critical condition for a healthy free society.

WORDS AND FACTS HAVE TO HAVE STABLE MEANING

For a free society to exist, people have to be able to talk with each other and consider who they are, what they want to do, what the priorities of a free society should be. To be able to so talk with each other in any sort of meaningful way, the words people use have to have stable and agreed-upon meaning. As Richard Weaver argues, the name of something is "not a convention which can be repealed by majority vote at the next meeting."[21] Lewis Carroll's Humpty Dumpty says much the same:

> "When *I* use a word," Humpty Dumpty said, in a rather scornful tone, "it means just what I choose it to mean—neither more nor less."
>
> "The question is," said Alice, "whether you *can* make words mean s o many different things."
>
> "The question is," said Humpty Dumpty, "which is to be master—that's all."[22]

Once we let words lose their meanings, anything goes. Jung Chang writes of what happened to language and words in China during the late 1950s: "Words became divorced from reality, responsibility, and people's real thoughts. Lies were told with ease because words had lost their meanings—and had ceased to be taken seriously by others."[23]

Facts, too, can lose their meanings. When one set of facts can be dismissed out of hand, to be replaced by a fantasized set of facts, it is difficult to maintain a free society: instead of facts on which to base thoughtful consideration of the world, we have power as the arbiter. When, in 1984, Winston Smith is tortured into agreeing that two plus two equals five if that is what Big Brother says, then all is surely lost.

Facts matter. In novels, in past times, down to our own time. When a relatively small crowd at a presidential inauguration is deemed by the incoming president to be the largest in the history of the country—in direct contradiction of the facts provided by photographs—and when his administration staff readily agrees to promulgate the new set of "facts" despite the obvious lying going on, then we are lost.

In defending British soldiers accused of perpetrating what became known as the Boston Massacre, John Adams concluded with this reminder: "Facts are stubborn things; and whatever may be our wishes, our inclinations, or the dictates of our passions, they cannot alter the state of facts and evidence."[24]

RESPECT FOR CIVIL DISCOURSE

If people find it impossible to talk with each other, advance ideas, adduce evidence, and weigh and consider options without resorting to verbal or physical violence, it will be difficult to sustain a free society. We must find ways for people to be able to talk. As with Pericles in his Funeral Oration: "Instead of looking on discussion as a stumbling-block in the way of action, we think it an indispensable preliminary to any wise action at all."[25] As people retreat more and more into themselves or into groups that maintain similar views, especially through various social media venues, it becomes easier and easier to reject civil discourse—in fact to reject any kind of discourse—in favor of an in-group tribalism and a rejection of those we presume will disagree with us.

An example of retreat can be seen in the response of many conservatives to the results of the November 2020 presidential election. As reported in the *New York Times*, "millions" have left fact-checked Facebook and Twitter and "migrated to alternative social media and media sites" in order to stay with news sources and with like-minded folk who will reinforce their views.[26]

Early on, it was thought that the development of various social media such as Twitter would lead to expanded democracy and civil discourse, with millions having opportunities to talk and exchange ideas. Instead, people using social media have tended to retreat even further into themselves or into like-minded groups. Social media allows for the immediate and indiscriminate spread of gossip and personal attacks. Guaranteed anonymity there is, but that anonymity leads to irresponsibility, with no need to be accountable to anybody for anything one says. The result, as Evgeny Morozov has suggested, is less civil discourse.[27]

FREE AND OPEN INQUIRY

People will not be able to participate in any thoughtful way in a free society unless they have the ability and the inclination to inquire into all aspects of their society and the world. They must be free to do so, without harm or threats. We must encourage critical inquiry—and the conditions associated with critical inquiry. We must encourage a willingness to be in the minority, even a minority of one, and we must, as John Dewey said, recognize the "capacity of the intelligence of the common man to respond with commonsense to the free play of facts and ideas which are secured by effective guarantees of free inquiry, free assembly, and free communication."[28]

RECOGNITION OF THE DIFFERENCE BETWEEN A PERSUADED AUDIENCE AND A MORE THOUGHTFUL PUBLIC

We need to understand the differences between "persuaded" and "more thoughtful" as well as differences between "audience" and "public." An audience, as we are considering here, can be seen as a passive recipient of messages of persuasion, while a public, especially one more thoughtful, will be an aware community, active and alert and more than willing to look into things and look askance at things.

A thoughtful public is careful, contemplative, aware of its rights and responsibilities, willing to think about matters with a view to the future as well as the present, and willing to consider issues and proposed actions in relation to other issues and actions as well as how those matters bear on the fundamental moral and political grounding of the whole. Further, an audience can be distinguished from a public in terms of interaction: Members of an audience tend to have little interaction with each other (and limited interaction with those who have called the audience together) while members of a public tend to have a lot of interaction with each other.

ECOLOGICAL UNDERSTANDING

As Gregory Bateson stressed, when considering the survival of any organism, the unit of survival is organism plus environment.[29] A fish can survive, but only in water, and only when the temperature of the water is between a given range; temperatures outside the range mean death for the fish. In like manner, no society, and certainly no free society, exists in a vacuum unconnected to anything else. The society is always nested in its larger environment, interacting with the variables in that larger environment. The only way for the society to survive is for the larger environment to survive.

For Bateson, the corollary is that the organism that destroys its environment destroys itself. The fish does not have the power to destroy its environment. But human beings, for better or worse, have that power and can cause not only the death of the fish but can threaten the environment of all living things and thus all societies.

It is clear that we need to consider with care how to use that power. We are confronted, like it or not, with the phenomenon of climate change. Climate change, in its various aspects, poses many threats to the environment and thus to ourselves. We need to deal with lethal heat, forest and brush fires, water pollution, depleted food production, rising sea levels, mass population displacement, and much more. Civilization may not end, as per some of the scenarios, but much more of our already scarce resources will have to be devoted to the climate change problems and thus significantly less will be available for education, health care, care of the elderly, and other essential goods and services.

ABILITY TO COUNTER THREATS TO A FREE SOCIETY

There is no guarantee that a free society will last forever. Free societies come and go; they can fade, die away. The always-perilous state of a free society is reflected in titles of recent studies and warnings: *How Democracies Perish*, *The Road to Unfreedom*, *How Democracy Ends*, *How Democracies Die*, *Twilight of Democracy*.[30]

Threats to a free society can come from without or within, and the threats can be posed by force or by inaction. Outside enemies can be an overwhelming existential threat. As we have seen many dreary times, it is all too easy for an invading army to eliminate the necessary conditions of a free society. Within a free society, a coup d'état or a military junta can eliminate by force the necessary conditions. A free society can try to counter the force with more of the same, while at the same time moving the enabling conditions into hiding until such time that the tyrannical force is defeated.

Free societies are less likely to be threatened by force: the threats more commonly stem from inattention and not caring about what it takes to sustain what one has. In his usual prescient way, Tocqueville warns us of the kind of despotism that might easily replace a free society. He suggests that the singular focus on "procuring the small and vulgar pleasures without which they fill their souls" will distract a free people from attending to the maintenance of their freedom. We are willing to buy in, Tocqueville suggests, as long as we think we are protected by the government to pursue our desired goods; whatever else the government does is of little consequence or is unthought of.[31]

The threats, then, more likely come from ourselves and our unwillingness to understand and secure and sustain the necessary conditions that enable our free society. What it takes to sustain and what it takes to destroy is the same; the only question is which side one wants to be on. For example, Machiavelli's *The Prince* is often seen as a guidebook showing what a prince needs to do—that is, what conditions are needed—to maintain power. Those seeing *The Prince* in this way tend to criticize Machiavelli as a supporter of tyranny. But a few readers have noted that the prescriptions for maintaining tyranny can be used as the guiding strategy for destroying tyranny.

UNDERSTANDING THAT THE POLITICAL PROCESS TAKES TIME

Any political project of any magnitude takes time. One must go from conception to getting on the agenda of political parties and gathering support. One must design enabling legislation and engage in effective persuasion, and upon enactment of legislation, one must develop rules and regulations and work through the beginnings of implementation. The political process is linked to the cultural leanings of a society, and culture often changes even more slowly than the political process. We can see the decades it has taken, for example, to achieve some modicum of progress in civil rights, women's rights, and the provision of health care.

It thus is sometimes tempting to give up on the political process in favor of showy projects that can be mounted in short order at relatively little cost. Tocqueville was aware of such temptations in France and in England. He warned his colleague, John Stuart Mill, about the costs of giving in: France and England should "not build railroads," he said, as compensation for not dealing with the deeper problems each nation was facing.[32]

A free society depends on a citizenry that eschews the quick-and-dirty show. Moreover, that citizenry will understand that the political process rarely yields absolute victory. In the reflective conclusion of *The Plague*, Camus reminds us that although the plague has been conquered in Oran, it was not a "final victory," and that what "had to be done . . . assuredly would have to be done again in the never ending fight against terror and its relentless onslaughts."[33] The political process takes time, is never finished, and any celebration of victory is at the same time a tocsin and reminder of the necessity to begin again. For a citizenry to so understand, a long-term view is necessary. It is that long-term view that we will address in greater detail in chapter 2.

PERSPECTIVES ON THE CONDITIONS AND FREE SOCIETY

Considered here are two perspectives on how we might approach the world and life in a free society. The first perspective deals with what people need to know about how to know the world. The second perspective deals with the nature of politics as the art of the possible and how the art of the possible might be in conflict with the ethical question of whether it is necessary to do the right things for the right reasons.

These two perspectives could be seen as conditions for a free society. But at the same time, they speak more broadly to matters dealing with working effectively in the world. The two perspectives speak to the political and the cultural, but also move further toward the philosophical.

WHAT PEOPLE NEED TO KNOW ABOUT HOW TO KNOW THE WORLD

Citizens in a free society have to be their own judges. To be good judges, they have to know a lot: they have to be able to sift through lots of data, make assessments of what is probable, and not be taken in by con artists of all kinds. Even under the best of circumstances, it is a challenging job, this determining how to see the world and how it works. And when under pressure—too much data, too little time, a multiplicity of interconnected variables, increasing numbers of politicians and other leaders willing to lie without compunction or shame, and immense information systems capable of generating and transmitting data instantaneously without regard to truth values—the challenge of making sound judgments is at once of even greater importance and less likely to be met.

Small wonder that under these sorts of pressures, many people are likely to become perplexed, and thus likely to believe whatever is convenient or fanciful or confirming of one's suspicions.

We are surely not the first to feel perplexed, or the first to let down our guard and welcome the fanciful over a search for the truth. In an extended and penetrating analysis, Ralph Lerner considers another group of people, the Jews of Yemen in the late twelfth century. Under all sorts of threats and pressures, in their confusion they are losing a careful sense of the world and are coming to believe all sorts of nonsense.

A rabbi in Yemen seeks guidance from Moses Maimonides, the one man who has the wisdom and practical knowledge to provide guidance for the confused people. In 1172, Maimonides responds with the Epistle to Yemen. It is the circumstances leading to the request and the response Maimonides gives that provide the basis for Lerner's commentary.

At issue is the matter of credulity. Lerner begins his commentary by considering the general tendency of people to believe, a tendency noted by another philosopher, Adam Smith, in 1759. Smith observes that it is natural for children to believe whatever they are told. Unquestioning belief is useful to protect the young from harm. As we ourselves know, we want our children to believe the hot stove is dangerous, and we don't want our children to disbelieve us and seek empirical evidence on their own.

The challenge, Smith says, is to gradually move the young from unquestioning belief to a good healthy skepticism. This movement is not easy to accomplish. "It is acquired wisdom and experience that teach incredulity, and they very seldom teach it enough. The wisest and most cautious of us all frequently gives credit to stories which he himself is afterwards both ashamed and astonished that he could possibly think of believing."[34]

It is that credulity, that propensity to believe anything, combined with a lack of ability to engage in critical thinking that Lerner suggests Maimonides sees in the beleaguered people of Yemen. In Maimonides's view, the people "lack some of the most fundamental skills for coping with the world. . . . They lack the indispensable criteria of sound judgment. They have not thought clearly about what might constitute good evidence. They have no systematic way of establishing the relevance of a particular observation. They have not addressed questions of probability. Further, they seem to lack even some basic notions of Nature. With some or all of these shortcomings, they can be led to believe anything" and "are vulnerable to confidence men of every kind."[35]

Further, it can be seen that "Ordinary people need to be weaned from their extravagant fantasies of an utterly plastic universe. As long as they think this world lacks form and is opaque to analysis, they will probably believe that they live in a place where anything can and does happen—magically, miraculously. . . . People need rather to recognize what philosophy has shown: that there is a world with a stable nature. That there are distinct species, each with its own purpose and perfection. That this world is subject to orderly, systematic investigation by science. That not everything calling itself science *is* science. That there are limits to human understanding and human efficacy. That there are criteria of credibility based on certain notions of evidence and probability. That large claims not only may but must be judged by those criteria lest the people be seduced into abandoning a solid truth for a will-o'-the-wisp."[36]

The people can work out of the muddle they are in, but the work will not be easy. As Lerner notes, "ultimately their redemption from error lies not in adopting a ready-made teaching but in their painstaking investment in genuine learning on their own behalf."[37]

In our time, we need ways of thinking, practical knowledge of how to know the world and live effectively. Although part of that knowledge might be applicable in all kinds of regimes, we need to understand that the skills of thinking and coping needed for citizens in a free society are markedly different from those needed for a non-free society. To survive as a subject in Stalinist Russia, one needed to keep quiet, assume a facade of total obedience, lie a lot, and appear to question nothing. But to be citizens in a free society, we need the same kinds of philosophical and practical knowledge outlined by Maimonides some 850 years ago. How we and successive generations might obtain that knowledge is discussed further in chapter 5.

THE ART OF THE POSSIBLE VERSUS DOING THE RIGHT THING FOR THE RIGHT REASON

Politics, it is sometimes said, is the art of the possible. Or, put another way by the Rolling Stones, you don't always get what you want, but sometimes you get what you need. There are many times when we compromise, learn to live with what we were able to work out, we give a little to get a little. It is not a perfect world we live in, where everybody gets exactly what they want. It's difficult to get everybody in a family to agree on what to have for dinner or where to go out for dinner. We agree to a job offer, even though we anticipate not getting all the benefits and working conditions we had hoped for. And surely if we cannot agree on dinner, and if we know we always have to compromise in getting a job, it is all the more likely we will never secure total agreement about the rightness of any proposed political action.

We accept that politics is indeed the art of the possible. After all, things have to get done. Budgets have to be approved so that essential public services can go on. We know that to hold out for every last little bit of perfection will likely result in not getting anything at all. And so we accept compromise.

But our willingness to compromise usually only extends so far. Compromise doesn't mean, we hope, amoral expediency. Our judgment of compromise in order to do the right thing as much as possible is tempered by the perennial question ethicists raise: is it necessary to do the right thing for the right reasons? Put another way, will doing the right thing for the wrong reasons ultimately mean we haven't done the right thing?

A plain hypothetical example illustrates the implications of how we respond to these questions. Suppose your child asks, "Why should I love Grandma?" And suppose you reply, "Because your Grandma is very rich and, if you are nice to her, she will leave a lot of money to you in her will." That's one reply, one proffered reason. Or, another reply: "Because she's your Grandma." Note that the behavior advocated is the same—loving Grandma. But note the implications of the two justifications or reasons you offer your child. To give the reason of getting money tells the child that this is how the world works: it's a calculative world, people do whatever in order to get a monetary payoff. On the other hand, saying to your child that you love Grandma purely because she is your Grandma is to offer a view of a normative world, a world in which one does things, at least sometimes, because it is the right thing to do.

We can see that doing the right thing for the wrong reason (assuming we think loving Grandma for a money payoff is wrong) ultimately means not only that we do not have the right reason, but also that the right behavior is somehow tarnished, something less than love. We end up with neither right thing nor right reason. Let us consider two examples of politics of the possible in light of the right things for right reasons question.

Our first example considers how women managed, after years of struggle, to get into medical school in America in the late 1800s. For years, women had been denied admission as a matter of formal policy. For many reasons, all specious, women were denied. New approaches were needed to eliminate the barriers.

One approach was suggested by Dr. Mary Jacobi, a leading physician, drawing on her experiences with French medical schools. In France, she had purchased "a number of concessions in gaining access to facilities open only to male students." At the first meeting of the Association for the Advancement of Women in 1875, Dr. Jacobi recommended the quid pro quo, dollars for admissions. "It is astonishing how many invincible objections on the score of feasibility, modesty, propriety, and prejudice will melt away before the charmed touch of a few thousand dollars."[38]

Harvard Medical School was chosen as a reasonable place to begin. The President of Harvard, Charles Eliot, seemed willing to consider an offer. In 1879, an offer was made: $10,000 in exchange for women to be admitted to medical school on equal terms with men. The offer was duly considered and rejected by the faculty, although a majority of the faculty did suggest that if Eliot were to go ahead, "Harvard should demand no less than a $200,000 endowment."[39] A group of women, including Dr. Jacobi, began raising the money. But by 1885, President Eliot had other priorities to deal with. The women turned their attention to Johns Hopkins University and its "financially beleaguered" new medical school. In the end, women were admitted—at a cost of $500,000.[40] A tidy sum now, even tidier in 1894.

It may be edifying to think of a group of women who had figured out how to work the system, how to get what they wanted. But the reasons for admittance of women had nothing to do with recognizing the wrongness of denying women simply because they were women. The barriers were removed, not for moral reasons, but for financial reasons: Johns Hopkins wanted the money. Johns Hopkins did the right thing, but, we can very well argue, for the wrong reasons.

Our second example of the art of the possible versus the ethical question of doing the right things for the right reasons comes from our own time. Many states in America have found it difficult to secure adequate monies for public schools. Despite pious and sometimes stentorian talk about the importance of schools, support is often difficult to find. During the last four decades, state lotteries have become a popular source of school funding. People buy lottery tickets, hoping to hit the jackpot. A portion of the lottery sales proceeds goes into the state's general fund, earmarked for the public schools. Here we have the art of the possible: getting money for schools from people who—at least many of them—would be unlikely to support school levies.

There is a cost, however, of not doing the right thing for the right reasons. Schools may get the funding, or at least a good portion of it, because of the lottery. But people are not supporting the schools in an active and knowing way. There is a considerable difference between buying a lottery ticket in order to perhaps win the jackpot while being at most vaguely aware that some of your purchase money will go for schools and voting, along with your fellow citizens, to support the schools. To say that "we need to tax ourselves a goodly amount for schools because it is important for children to get a good education and it is important that they learn how to become good and responsible citizens in a free society" is considerably different than saying "give me twenty dollars' worth of lottery tickets and let's hope this time I'm lucky."

If people don't consciously choose to tax themselves for schools, it's not likely that schools will last for very long, other than in some barebones pro forma way, and when the supposedly painless lottery is abandoned (for whatever reason), lottery ticket buyers are not going to have an epiphany and realize that schools are important and worthy of self-taxation.

There is no formulaic way out of the tension between politics as the art of the possible and the need to do the right things for the right reasons. Nor should there be, because we need the tension, we need both perspectives. The best we can do, which is the necessary thing to do, is try to keep the tension before us. There are times when getting something done might be seen as more important than having all of our moral criteria being met. And there are times when we will feel compelled by our own moral sense that it matters little whether something is possible or not, because not always is possibility its own justification.

We have proffered fifteen conditions necessary for a free society and two perspectives bearing on the world and how we need to know and behave in that world. The list could be extended, reduced, otherwise altered. However altered, there must be some sort of collection of conditions and ways of viewing the world if we are to indeed have and deserve and sustain a free society. Leaders play vital roles in helping to create and sustain conditions; those roles are discussed in chapter 3. We all, as citizens, play a vital role, as discussed in chapter 4. And given that sustaining a free society means that the young need to be taught to understand and value the conditions and perspectives, attention must be paid to matters of education and schools, as discussed in chapter 5.

NOTES

1. Harold Lasswell, *Politics: Who Gets What, When, How?* (New York: McGraw-Hill, 1936).
2. James Madison, *Federalist* No. 51, in *The Federalist*, ed. Jacob E. Cooke (Middletown, Conn.: Wesleyan University Press, 1961), 349.
3. Ralph Lerner, *The Thinking Revolutionary: Principle and Practice in the New Republic* (Ithaca: Cornell University Press, 1987), 61.
4. Alexis de Tocqueville, *Democracy in America*, trans. Harvey C. Mansfield and Delba Winthrop (Chicago: University of Chicago Press, 2000), 275.
5. Francis Fukuyama, *Trust: The Social Virtues and the Creation of Prosperity* (New York: Free Press, 1995). See also Bernard Barber, *The Logic and Limits of Trust* (New Brunswick, N.J.: Rutgers University Press, 1983).
6. Peter Baker, "Dishonesty Has Defined the Trump Presidency. The Consequences Could Be Lasting," *New York Times*, November 1, 2020. https://www.nytimes.com/2020/11/01/us/politics/trump-presidency-dishonesty.html.
7. James Farr, "Social Capital," *Political Theory* 32, no. 1 (February 2004). See also Robert D. Putnam, *Making Democracy Work: Civic Traditions in Modern Italy* (Princeton: Princeton University Press, 1993) along with Robert D. Putnam, *Bowling Alone* (New York: Simon & Schuster, 2000). An earlier formulation can be found in James Coleman, *Foundations of Social Theory* (Cambridge, Mass.: Belknap Press, 1990), 300–321.
8. Patrick Brown, "The Dark Side of Social Capital," *National Affairs* 40 (Summer 2019).
9. Herbert J. Muller, *Issues of Freedom: Paradoxes and Promises* (New York: Harper & Brothers, 1960), 5.
10. Herodotus, *The Persian Wars*, trans. George Rawlinson, bk. 7, ch. 135 (New York: Modern Library, 1942), 547.
11. Herbert J. Muller, *Freedom in the Western World: From the Dark Ages to the Rise of Democracy* (New York: Harper & Row, 1963), 301.
12. James Van Horn Melton, *Absolutism and the Eighteenth-Century Origins of Compulsory Schooling in Prussia and Austria* (Cambridge: Cambridge University Press, 1988), 212, 216.
13. Leo Strauss, *Persecution and the Art of Writing* (1952; reprint, Chicago: University of Chicago Press, 1988), 37.
14. George Washington, *The Writings of George Washington*, ed. J. C. Fitzpatrick, vol. 30 (Washington, D.C.: Government Printing Office, 1939), 493.
15. Thomas Jefferson, "Notes on Virginia," in *Writings* (New York: Library of America, 1984), 274. For the proposed school legislation, see Thomas Jefferson, "Revisal of the Laws, Bill no. 79, A Bill for the More General Diffusion of Knowledge," in *Writings* (New York: Library of America, 1984), 365–73.
16. Ralph Lerner, *Revolutions Revisited: Two Faces of the Politics of Enlightenment* (Chapel Hill: University of North Carolina Press, 1994), 43.
17. Washington, *Writings*, 493.
18. Lerner, *Thinking Revolutionary*, 25.

19. Philip B. Kurland and Ralph Lerner, eds., *The Founders' Constitution*, vol. 1 (Chicago: University of Chicago Press, 1987), 424.

20. Tocqueville, *Democracy in America*, 501–2.

21. Richard Weaver, "Language is Sermonic" in *Language Is Sermonic: Richard M. Weaver on the Nature of Rhetoric*, eds. Richard L. Johannesen, Rennard Strickland, and Ralph T. Eubanks (Baton Rouge: Louisiana State University Press, 1970), 192–93.

22. Lewis Carroll, *Through the Looking Glass* (New York: Collier, 1962), 247.

23. Jung Chang, *Wild Swans: Three Daughters of China* (New York: Doubleday, 1991), 225.

24. John Adams, "Adams' Argument for the Defense: 3–4 December 1770," *Founders Online,* National Archives, https://founders.archives.gov/documents/Adams/05-03-02-0001-0004-0016.

25. Thucydides, *The Peloponnesian War*, trans. Richard Crawley (New York: Modern Library, 1951), 105.

26. Mike Isaac and Kellen Browning, "Fact-Checked on Facebook and Twitter," *New York Times*, November 11, 2020, https://www.nytimes.com/2020/11/11/technology/parler-rumble-newsmax.html?searchResultPosition=1.

27. Evgeny Morozov, *The Net Delusion: The Dark Side of Internet Freedom* (New York: PublicAffairs, 2012).

28. John Dewey, "Creative Democracy—The Task before Us," in *John Dewey: The Later Works, 1925–1953, vol. 14, 1939–1941*, ed. Jo Ann Boydston (Carbondale: Southern Illinois University Press, 1988), 227.

29. Gregory Bateson, *Steps to an Ecology of Mind* (New York: Ballantine, 1972; reissued with a foreword by Mary Catherine Bateson, Chicago: University of Chicago Press, 2000).

30. See Jean-Francois Revel, *How Democracies Perish* (New York: Doubleday, 1983); Timothy Snyder, *The Road to Unfreedom: Russia, Europe, America* (New York: Tim Duggan Books, 2018); David Runciman, *How Democracy Ends* (New York: Basic Books, 2018); Steven Levitsky and David Ziblatt, *How Democracies Die* (New York: Basic Books, 2018); and Anne Applebaum, *Twilight of Democracy: The Seductive Lure of Authoritarianism* (New York: Doubleday, 2020).

31. Tocqueville, *Democracy in America*, 661–65.

32. See Alexis de Tocqueville, "To John Stuart Mill, March 18, 1841," in *Selected Letters on Politics and Society*, ed. Roger Boesche, trans. James Toupin and Roger Boesche (Berkeley: University of California Press, 1985), 150–51.

33. Albert Camus, *The Plague*, trans. Stuart Gilbert (New York: Knopf, 1980), 278.

34. Adam Smith, *The Theory of Moral Sentiments*, vol. 1 of *The Glasgow Edition of the Works and Correspondence of Adam Smith*, ed. D. D. Raphael and A. L. Macfie (1976; reprint, Indianapolis: Liberty Fund, 1982).

35. Ralph Lerner, *Maimonides' Empire of Light: Popular Enlightenment in an Age of Belief* (Chicago: University of Chicago Press, 2000), 7–8.

36. Lerner, *Maimonides' Empire*, 9–10.

37. Lerner, *Maimonides' Empire*, 9.

38. Mary Roth Walsh, *Doctors Wanted: No Women Need Apply: Sexual Barriers in the Medical Profession, 1835–1975* (New Haven: Yale University Press, 1977), 169.
39. Walsh, *Doctors Wanted*, 172.
40. Walsh, *Doctors Wanted*, 177.

Chapter 2

Long-Term Perspective in a Free Society

From birth on, we have an acute sense of time. A baby is hungry, looking for food right now, and has no tolerance for waiting. Time is now. As we grow older, we still want a lot of things right now. Our wanting is still there, but we learn that the holidays won't come any faster by crying. We begin to develop some sense of time not yet here, the future. And, as we grow older, time becomes a big part of what we do and experience. Schools are where time sense emerges as important.

For some of us, elementary school grades were assigned for learning, for effort, and for punctuality. One might think of other aspects of behavior that educators might have deemed important enough to single out and somehow grade—kindness or skill at authentically listening to others, for example. But those were left aside. Being on time took one of the three top spots. At school, we learned, one is either on time or one is tardy. Bells ring, we have ten minutes before getting to the next class, another opportunity to be on time or tardy.

The sense of time—the importance of time and how we perceive time and deal with it—continues to develop throughout our life. There are things we plan to do and things we realize we won't have time to do. We set aside savings, plan our future, our retirement. Time is certainly with us in all we do. Time is so prevalent for us that the word "time" is the most common noun in the English language.[1]

And we surely become aware of the finiteness of time. The shot clock winding down. Perhaps we are moving a bit beyond the Biblical span of life—three score and ten—to a longer span. Ninety years, even for an increasing number of us, the century mark. Even with that increase, we are aware that our time on Earth is finite, limited.

The many aspects of the psychology and philosophy of time are fascinating and have secured the attention of poets, philosophers, psychologists, all of us.[2] For our purposes here, however, we narrow our discussion of time to a limited field, namely, a consideration of short-term time perspectives and long-term time perspectives. We know that we all make distinctions between what we think is a "short time" and a "long time" from now. And we know people vary in terms of their sense of what is short and what is long. What we need to consider is whether short-term and long-term time perspectives somehow bear on securing and sustaining a healthy free society. Is there a relationship? If so, why is the relationship important?

What follows is a consideration of prevalent short-term time experiences, both in terms of individual and corporate perspectives. We then consider the negative implications of short-term time and discuss why, if short-termism has so many downsides, it is still so prevalent. We then turn to a discussion of why a long-term time perspective is necessary for a free society and conclude with a discussion of what it will take to make the shift from a short-term to a long-term perspective.

SHORT TERM, LONG TERM: INDIVIDUAL AND CORPORATE PERSPECTIVES

In so many ways, Alexis de Tocqueville had astonishing insights into the American political and social scene derived from his famous visit in 1830–1831. His *Democracy in America* remains the most quoted book about America on dozens of topics: government, politics, equality, tyranny of the majority, as well as culture and folkways.

Given the importance of time conceptions, it doesn't come as a surprise that Tocqueville devotes a chapter to how he sees Americans managing time. It is a haunting, melancholic chapter, starting with the chapter title: "Why the Americans Show Themselves So Restive in the Midst of Their Well-Being." Here are "the freest and most enlightened men placed in the happiest condition that exists in the world." But "a sort of cloud habitually covers their features; they appeared to me grave and almost sad even in their pleasures."

He speaks of the "feverish ardor" with which Americans pursue prosperity, how "they show themselves constantly tormented by a vague fear of not having chosen the shortest route that can lead to it." The typical American "is always in a hurry," always imagining thousands of goods that "death will prevent him from enjoying if he does not hasten." The thought of missing out "fills him with troubles, fears, and regrets, and keeps his soul in a sort of unceasing trepidation."[3]

The short-term time perspective that Tocqueville observed was derived in part from the desire for material goods, for prosperity, for some sort of pursuit of happiness, and over the some 180 years since Jacksonian times, the desire and pursuit have not abated. We want the better car, or a second or third car, a better house, more vacations, a higher standard of living. We want these for ourselves now, while keeping an eye on what we want for our children, and with Tocqueville, we know we have a limited time and will look for and favor the most direct path to achieving our goals in the time we have left.

Our experience of stress, of pressure, of being in a hurry is made even more compelling by the reminders that come from the constant reminders of the ever-increasing speed of things in the world. Computers and the internet are everywhere a constant part of our lives. We communicate almost instantaneously through social media. While in some years past we might wait a week for a response to a letter we sent by, as one would say now, snail mail, we expect our emails to be responded to within minutes.

There are great, almost unfathomable increases in speed of information transmission. And there are similar increases in the amount of information available. It is estimated that the internet "is already made of one quintillion transistors, a trillion links, a million emails per second, 20 exabytes of memory."[4]

It is small wonder that given our short-term time perspective and the speeding up of greatly increased amounts of information that we feel, as one book title has it, pressed for time,[5] or that we live in, as per by another book title, empires of speed. And perhaps, taking a breath during a brief pause, we can think of William Wordsworth and his observation that "the world is too much with us, getting and spending, we lay waste our powers." Wordsworth suggests, as with Tocqueville, that we are "out of tune" with the world.[6]

One response to the short-term frame and perceived lack of time is to do better at time management. There are many books on the self-help shelf to help us do just that. A typical entry here is Ashley Whillans' recent book, *Time Smart: How to Reclaim Your Time and Live a Happier Life*.[7] One gets a certain relief just by lingering over the subtitle.

Or, if we perceive there isn't enough time, there is an antidote for the taking: create more time by slowing down. And again, there are many suggestions of ways we can do just that, such as those noted by Carl Honoré, *In Praise of Slowness: Challenging the Culture of Speed*.[8] There are indeed some advantages gained by going slow, as Honoré: one can feel better, less harried, more appreciative of the world.

And some advantages can be seen by direct observation. Consider, for example, pedestrian traffic patterns shown between classes on any large college campus. There are lots of people crisscrossing, walking from one building to another in all sorts of directions. Very rarely do people run into each other. That's because everybody is moving comparatively slowly, and minor adjustments in direction and speed can be made with little effort. Were these same people to try to cross a freeway, they would be killed. There is little opportunity to make adjustments while driving at seventy miles per hour. Likewise, some executives in organizations find that if they put things on a slower pace, they are able to make the minor adjustments that keep morale and productivity high.

It should be noted, too, that calling attention to the phenomena of increased data and increased data speed does not mean that there is anything inherently wrong with having lots of data at ever-increasing speed. But we should not on principle deny use of data simply because of data speed or because of the possibilities of ill-use. The challenge is to maintain control over how we approach things, how we use the data to better understand the world, to make better decisions.

The ways we have been talking about so far focus on the individual and how the individual short-term time perspective and the individual response to the perceived pressures of not having enough time. The focus, it should be stressed, is on the individual, how the individual cannot be overwhelmed. There is little in the you-against-time self-help literature to suggest a concern with the larger community, the commonweal, the free society. The self-help prescriptions for behavior leave intact and unspoken the prevalent short-term time perspective.

As with individuals, many American businesses operate from a short-term time perspective. The emphasis for many businesses has long been on the quarterly report, quarterly earnings, quarterly profits—in effect, what has been called quarterly capitalism.

One acute observer of the short-termism, Dominic Barton, argues that the "mania over quarterly earnings consumes extraordinary amounts of senior time and attention," and "even philanthropy often exhibits a fetish for the short term and the new, with grantees expected to become self-sustaining in just a few years."[9] Barton claims that executives "excessively discount long-term cash flows in favour of easier to quantify short-term metrics such as quarterly earnings."[10]

The focus on short-termism has received increased interest by economists and other financial analysts in the past twenty years, an increased interest in the possible downsides of the short-term perspective. A 2006 study of some executives in four hundred companies found that 78 percent of those surveyed would support sacrificing their corporation's economic value in order to meet quarterly earnings expectations.[11]

As suggested by another analyst, the corporate executives are not alone in helping to sacrifice the long-term for the short-term gain. "There's a growing culture of analysts and traders obsessing over a company's quarterly performance and panicking if a company posts poor quarterly results. This culture has been enabled by the availability of information about companies on the Internet and television."[12]

It is not only businesses that buy into the short term. Some school districts appear to want to take what is thought to be the shortest possible path to goal achievement at the expense of the long-term development of value. In 2009, some 180 Atlanta School District administrators and teachers were charged with altering student answers on high-stakes academic achievement tests.[13]

There are some executives and organizations that have begun to speak in favor of a long-term perspective. Amazon's CEO Jeff Bezos has argued that part of his corporation's success is due to an eschewing of the short term (which Bezos pegs as three years) in favor of the long term (seven years).[14] The Bezos long-term span of seven years is similar to what Barton suggests: "for a rough definition of 'long term,' think of the time required to invest in and build a profitable new business, which McKinsey suggests is five to seven years."[15]

Thus, those wishing to conduct a serious conversation about the need for a "long-term perspective" will have to avoid the abstract and move to positive terms. Seven years might be an appropriate "long term" for corporations—perhaps. But surely seven years cannot be considered "long term" in, say, the context of determination of public policy in response to climate change.

As with any kind of analysis, there is not total agreement as to the prevalence and danger of short-termism.[16] Nonetheless, organizations have been formed to advocate for a long-term perspective and to counter the short term. One such is FCLTGlobal. Founded in 2013 by McKinsey & Company as Focusing Capital on the Long Term, the nonprofit expanded three years later to include member organizations from nine countries as a "do tank, not a think tank" to provide practical tools and support for business executives, asset owners, and fund managers.[17]

Another is the American Prosperity Project, a part of the Aspen Institute. The project, a "nonpartisan framework for policy action," focuses on increasing jobs and productivity through expanded long-term investment in infrastructure as well as changing the corporate tax structure, given that "short-termism is baked into our tax system." The overall aim is "the restoration of public trust in capitalism itself as an economic system that works for all."[18]

The concerted efforts of such organizations as FCLTGlobal and American Prosperity Project suggest that short-term perspectives appear to be difficult to alter. If it were easy to go from short-termism to the long term, then the many persistent efforts would not be all necessary.

We noted that individuals trying to accommodate short-term perspectives through various time management strategies tend to pay little attention to the larger political context or the needs of a free society. The efforts of some in the business community to shift from short-termism to a long-term perspective often have a similar narrow focus. The argument is that having a long-term perspective will make it more likely that a corporation can enjoy increased profits and productivity, and the efforts to make the shift are rarely argued in terms of impact on the conduct of a free society, politics, government. Indirectly, the shift to a long (or at least somewhat longer) term might well support a healthier free society. To have business focus exclusively on the short term while trying to enable other societal structures to focus on the long term makes little sense.

Political philosopher Sheldon Wolin argued that "political time is out of synch with the temporalities, rhythms, and pace governing economy and culture." He suggested that political action "must be preceded by deliberation and deliberation, as its "deliberate" part suggests, takes time because, typically, it occurs in a setting of competing or conflicting but legitimate considerations."[19]

Overall, though, despite some business efforts to move beyond the short term, we are left with the finding of the Oxford Martin Commission for Future Generations. In its final report, the commission cited "embedded short-termism" as a major factor threatening the development of effective responses to critical global challenges, suggesting that "electoral cycles, media pressures, company reporting timetables and just-in-time systems encourage short-sightedness" and that "today's leaders seem increasingly distracted by 24/7 media pressures, election timetables and the 'urgency of now.'"[20]

DISADVANTAGES OF SHORT-TERM TIME PERSPECTIVES FOR A FREE SOCIETY

As discussed in chapter 1, a free society, like all societies, has to be constantly concerned with the basics of the political process, that is, who gets what and why. There is never enough for all, there is always the question of how to allocate scarce resources. Problems must be stated in appropriate ways, alternatives proposed, solutions decided on and implemented and subsequently evaluated. Priorities must be established, only to be revisited as a result, perhaps, of the appearance of new information regarding competing priorities.

Not only do we have to conduct thoughtful analyses, we have to pay close attention to the process itself: citizens from a great variety of backgrounds and perspectives must be engaged in authentic participation in the deliberative and analytical process. Political leaders, their staff, and those with scientific expertise may well be equipped in part to seek and analyze relevant data in multivariate ways, but a public—a more thoughtful public—must play a major role.

There are many disadvantages posed by a short-term perspective when trying to achieve better thinking, better deliberation, and better outcomes in a free society. Following is a discussion of five of the major disadvantages.

The first disadvantage is that we are so focused on getting it all right now that we don't spend very much time thinking about the health of the free society. Tocqueville is again our guide. He suggested that as long as people "revolve on themselves without repose, procuring the small and vulgar pleasures with which they fill their souls," they will be unwilling to have much concern about their obligations as citizens in a free society.[21] People will focus on the short term, on what will be of immediate benefit to them, and as long as they feel the government will not stop them from getting the most they can as quickly as possible, they will not care what the government does.

A second disadvantage of the short-term perspective is the tendency to have bad or incorrect or limited analysis. The lack of time to consider, the rush to judgment, limits systems thinking, holistic thinking, multivariate analysis, the discouragement of understanding how variables are related. Problems tend to be defined narrowly.

In *The Clock of the Long Now*, Stewart Brand quotes Danny Hillis: "There are problems that are impossible if you think about them in two-year terms—which everyone does—but they are easy if you think in fifty-year terms."[22]

A third disadvantage of the short term is that we are likely to develop incorrect or inadequate understanding of analysis of research bearing on public policy.

Consider the Flexner Report on medical education and how to under stand its impact. In 1908, the Carnegie Foundation for the Advancement of Teaching asked Abraham Flexner to visit and evaluate all of the medical schools of the United States and Canada and to make recommendations for reforms as needed. Flexner did so and submitted his report in 1910.[23] It is generally considered one of the most influential pedagogical documents of the twentieth century. Many of the medical schools that Flexner deemed inadequate closed their doors. Others remained open but wanted to improve.

With the support of major foundations, Flexner and others undertook major projects over a period of decades to improve medical schools. A challenging task. From our current perspective, we can look back and conclude that the Flexner Report of 1910 had a major impact. Fortunately, over the decades, there were medical professionals and—just as important—foundation folks who were committed to staying the course of medical school reform.

But consider the Flexner Report in the short term. The report was issued in 1910. With a short-term perspective, foundation people in, say, 1917—seven years, the Bezos long term—might have evaluated the impact of the report and concluded that not much had changed in improving health care in America. Seen in a time frame of seven years, the Flexner Report would be a dud. It would not be until at least forty years later that the true impact of the report could be understood.

Another example of short-term time perspective leading to an incorrect or limited view of research findings can be found in *The Clock of the Long Now*: "A nine-year study in Africa concluded that burning new woody growth in open grassland could not prevent the woods from taking over. A forty-year study of the same subject proved the opposite, that annual burning was an ideal way to keep the grasslands open. It takes more than a decade of fires to keep woody rootstocks from resprouting, that's all."[24]

A fourth result of the short-term time perspective: It is difficult to have and maintain a more thoughtful public. As discussed in chapter 1, to be a more thoughtful public means to be reflective, to think things through. A thoughtful public is careful, aware of its rights and responsibilities, willing to contemplate matters with a view to the future as well as the present.

It is critical for the creation and maintenance of a more thoughtful public that there be adequate time to talk, to interact, to be with each other, to secure and sustain and pay attention to a public, a community. The process takes time. By taking time, we are doubly to the good: we are likely to come up with better analyses and solutions, and we are likely to better secure our more thoughtful public. Without enough time, with the pressure of a short-term time perspective, we are likely to shortchange and short circuit the process.

A fifth disadvantage of the short-term perspective is the tendency for rapid turnover of leaders, whether in government or the private sector. The short-term perspective nudges us to expect action and results coming on the near horizon, and we become impatient when those results are still far off. The average length of executive tenure continues to drop. Charles Eliot assumed the presidency of Harvard University in 1869. He was president for forty years, and his successor, Lawrence Lowell, thirty-four. Those long tenures, allowing for some long-term perspectives to be acted on, have vanished. Those who are part of the comparatively rapid executive turnover will tend to favor the short-term in order to get as much possible done before they are out the door.

The short-term perspective is pervasive, affecting those in businesses, in the schooling sector, in government. Although there are no formal linkages, those in these three major sectors of society appear to act in unison. We would find it odd to see long-term perspective prevail in one of the three and short-term perspective prevail in the other two. There seems to be here a kind of ecology of perspective, an ecology of time.

It should be noted that the disadvantages of short-term perspective are being considered in terms of a desired free society. These disadvantages don't obtain in the same way in a non-free society. Economist Mancur Olson suggests that dictators tend to define short term and political conduct in terms of how long they want to (or hope to) stay in power.[25] The concern about having a more thoughtful public is not a factor in a non-free society. Where would be the need for active citizen engagement in public policy matters? What kind of dictator would countenance such engagement?

We cannot imagine someone saying to Stalin, "Hey, Comrade Stalin, don't you think we need to think things through?" For that matter, we cannot imagine Stalin forming authentic (not rubber-stamp) citizens' committees to critique his plans. Stalin and the Bolsheviks did indeed have a bit of long-term thinking, what with the many Five-Year-Plans, but all of the production targets were derived from Stalin's expressed personal wishes.

The concern about problem definition is not a factor, because the dictator and some kind of central committee do the defining. Likewise, assessment of public policy and program evaluation are untouched by short-term perspectives in a non-free society because the results are whatever those in power say they are.

But for a free society, predominantly short-term time perspectives present major disadvantages. It is difficult enough to conduct good political processes in a free society under the best of circumstances. Short-term time perspectives severely limit the ability to act in thoughtful ways to thoughtful ends.

IF SHORT-TERM TIME PERSPECTIVE IS SO BAD, WHY DOES IT CONTINUE?

Why, if short-termism is so bad (at least for a free society), do we continue to have it? A partial response is that, as we have noted, the short-term perspective is what many (most?) people want. And thus the politicians we elect are similarly focused on the short term. They are focused on the short term for three reasons. First, the next election is always upon them. The pressure is particularly acute for politicians holding offices that have two-year terms, such as the House of Representatives. Even those holding elective offices of four-or six-year terms find that the clock is running, re-election committees must be organized, and fundraising efforts must, as always, be intensified.

A second reason why politicians focus on the short term is that politicians, and the rest of us, have a strong sense that any given political drift will not last long. When Lyndon Johnson was asked why he was not celebrating the huge presidential victory of November 1964, Johnson said that he knew Congress, and he knew that he had a very short window opening, a very short time in which to try to accomplish what he wanted, even though he had engineered a landslide victory and the Democrats had large majorities in both the House and Senate.[26]

A third reason why politicians focus on the short term is that they are responding to what they think constituents say they want. Constituents say they want tax cuts. Now. They want a new bridge built. Now. They don't want to pay for something they (or at most their children) won't be able to use.

When The Doors sang "we want the world and we want it . . . now," they were simply making manifest what was (and still is) a predominant cultural phenomenon. If we were to shift to a long-term perspective, it's a good bet that politicians would respond accordingly and would eschew the short-term perspective.

Another factor contributing to maintenance of short-term perspective is what Elise Boulding calls "temporal exhaustion." "If one is mentally out of breath all the time from dealing with the present, there is no energy left for imaging the future."[27]

The predominance of the short-term time perspective poses many disadvantages for a free society. What we have considered so far, directly and by implication, suggests that a long-term perspective obviates the disadvantages and has some requirements of its own. It is to an examination of the long term that we now turn.

THE NECESSITY OF A LONG-TERM PERSPECTIVE FOR A FREE SOCIETY

There are two ways to frame how to consider the bearing of a long-term time perspective on a free society. One way is to focus on the present, to consider the need for long-term perspective so as not to let a free society slip from us through complacency and sloppy ways of thinking (or not thinking at all). The other way is to focus on the need to sustain a free society over many generations by means of a long-term perspective to identify and weigh future possible variables and alternatives. Both ways of framing are necessary, and both are considered in turn.

It has been suggested that a political regime is made actual through "institutions, procedures, and habits of mind."[28] And, as suggested in chapter 1, a free society has as its citizenry a more thoughtful public, and not just a persuaded audience. One habit of mind critical to securing and sustaining a more thoughtful public as part of a free society is thoughtful discussion, analysis, and understanding prior to action. It takes time to be thoughtful. One has to gather and listen to a great deal of information, and even prior to that, one has to take a great deal of time to determine, individually and through working with others, just what information might be needed: delineation of information needs can take more time than the actual gathering of information.

Thoughtfulness also means seeing and attending to the interrelationships of many variables and considering those interrelationships not only in the immediate context, but in possible future contexts. There is little of much worth in life that can be gained by maximizing on a single variable, and even less to be gained by maximizing on a single variable exclusively in the immediate term and ignoring the long term.

Being more thoughtful necessarily includes persistent consideration of the long term. This is not to say that we should overlook or denigrate short-term outcomes, because sometimes those outcomes—in any organization, in any political situation—need to be on the immediate horizon.

But the process by which we achieve our ends is rarely unimportant. In many situations, process will—or should—take precedence over product, and if the process is rushed—short term, if you will—the product might well suffer, and there might well be unanticipated consequences as well.

Consider, for example, a school administrator who wants her teaching staff to develop and subsequently act on an agreed-upon set of school goals. The temptation is to do the job herself. After all, people in the business with some years of experience will be able to predict with reasonable accuracy the list of goals the teachers will specify. Our administrator could indeed develop a list of goals reasonably predictive of what the teachers will come up with. Why not save a lot of time, just give the teachers the list of goals, and get on with it?

The answer, of course, is that the people in any group have to work things out for themselves if there is to be any internalizing, any serious commitment. The process of goal identification might take a morning, it might take all day, or even longer. But in the end, the teachers are likely to have made the goals their own, and with ownership comes commitment, not just for the moment but over time. Yes, the list of goals is roughly the same as that which could have been laid out by the administrator. The great difference is not in the product but in the process. If the administrator generates the list, then the necessary task is to persuade the staff to adopt the list, and there is a reasonable chance that the staff will not adopt but rather will resent the attempted imposition.

What takes place in one school, as per our example, is replicated and re-enacted many times over in all parts of a free society. A free society needs a more thoughtful public. Thoughtfulness takes time, both to consider multiple variables in the long term and to enact processes that reinforce the very thoughtfulness that is necessary.

We can now consider the second perspective—the long-range perspective that is necessary in order to sustain a free society over time, over decades, over centuries. We need to understand that a free society does not exist in a vacuum. As with any society, a free society is nested in the larger environmental context. Gregory Bateson reminds us that the unit of survival for any organism is the organism *plus* its environment, not the organism *against* its environment: "the organism that destroys its environment destroys itself."[29] Attention must be paid to the larger environment. If the air is polluted, if the water is undrinkable or unavailable, if food supply is limited, then for us, for our immediate community, for our world, it will be very difficult to sustain a free society.

The long-term environmental problems we are facing—population growth, climate change, and more—demand a long-term perspective if we are to understand and deal with those problems in any substantive way. If these problems are not dealt with, then the very wealthy will continue business within literal and figurative gated communities, while the majority are left with a shallow and desperate existence. Hardly grounds for a healthy free society.

A healthy free society demands a long-term time perspective, the kind of perspective that is clearly in short supply. How, then, can we make the shift from the short term to the long term?

MAKING THE SHIFT FROM SHORT TERM TO LONG TERM

We have noted the disadvantages of the short-term perspective. And we have seen the importance of the long-range perspective for a healthy free society. Assuming we want to make the shift from the short term to the long term, where might we turn? What are some sources of support? Let us consider three sources for change: nonprofit organizations, schools, and—most important—ourselves.

Following are brief descriptions of two organizations that are trying to change our culture, help ease the shift to a long-term perspective. One such is the Long Now Foundation, a nonprofit San Francisco organization founded by Stewart Brand and others in 1996.[30] Stewart Brand has been involved in cultural change efforts for some half a century, starting with the publication of the Whole Earth Catalog. Space exploration photographs in the late 1960s showed the whole earth from afar. Brand used the images as a way to persuade people to think in terms of the connectedness of the whole. The Long Now Foundation works in similar ways to use imagery to persuade.

Perhaps the best known of the foundation's projects is the 10,000-year clock currently being constructed deep inside a mountain in west Texas. The clock is designed to tick for ten millennia with minimal maintenance, part of the effort to get people to think in the long term. Amazon's Jeff Bezos is providing major support—$42 million—for the clock project. What his involvement can suggest to us is that context is critical in considering views of what is meant by "long term." What might be considered appropriate long term in one context might not be appropriate in another. As noted earlier in this chapter, Bezos sees seven years as a long time in the context of his Amazon business. At the same time, Bezos can see a[#]long time in terms of millennia.

Another organization with an advocacy focus on the future is the London-based Long Time Project. The work centers on the role of culture, according to founders Ella Saltmarshe and Beatrice Pembroke. Culture is "foundational to the way science, politics, economics and technology develop. It shapes how we feel, how we emphasize and how we connect with each other. It provides the reflective space to navigate complexity and uncertainty." Three ideas guide the Long Time Project work: (1) "We need to feel an emotional connection to future generations"; (2) "Developing longer perspectives on our existence will change the way we behave in the short term"; and (3) "Art and culture will be crucial to cultivating long-term attitudes and behaviours."[31]

Both the Long Now Foundation and The Long Time Project assume the need for long-term cultural change. Neither engages in direct political action in the sense of supporting candidates, lobbying legislators on specific bills, or drafting rules and regulations. Both organizations have a view to the long term and see the culture underlying the political as their major target, assuming that as the culture changes for the better, the political will follow along.

There are other organizations that have addressed the problem of short-term perspective. One such organization, mentioned earlier in this chapter, is the Oxford Martin Commission for Future Generations. The commission, no longer in existence, pointed more directly to the political in its final report. The basic question addressed in the report, according to one observer, is "how can one persuade political actors—national governments, international organizations, corporations, and private citizens—to shift their frame of reference from immediate demands and present desires to the requirements of a stable, prosperous, and sustainable future?"[32] However, that same observer suggests, "If the report has a weakness, it is its lack of political realism. The commission acknowledges, at least implicitly, that all politics is local. And yet its ambitious agenda requires elected leaders to do the unprecedented: subordinate the immediate, particularistic interests of their constituents to long-term, global interests."

The commission's final report was issued in 2013. There has been some sentiment to find ways to continue its work through other venues. For example, in 2018 the Foundation for Democracy and Sustainable Development proposed that England's House of Lords "establish a Committee for Future

Generations to review legislation," in an effort to "reduce the short-termism that can creep into legislative and executive decision-making."[33]

Another effort to bring long-term time perspective directly into the political process was the Knesset Commission for Future Generations established in Israel in 2001. The mission was "enhancing long-term and sustainable thinking among policymakers and in the state of Israel at large and ensure that these considerations are included in primary and secondary legislation." The commission was abolished in 2006, apparently for cost reasons and claims of too much interference in the political process.[34]

Schools are the second source of possible support for making the shift from the short term to the long term. After all, if we want to effect this shift, not only for ourselves but for many people over many years, then it makes sense to consider what educators in schools could do. Although we will discuss in larger perspective the role of schools in sustaining a free society, a few observations can be made here regarding schools and time perspective.

A time perspective curriculum could be developed and shared among schools. The basic elements could follow the six topics Roman Krznaric suggests for a "cognitive toolkit." These six are:

1. Deep-Time Humility: grasp we are an eyeblink in cosmic time
2. Legacy Mindset: be remembered well by posterity
3. Intergenerational Justice: consider the seventh generation ahead
4. Cathedral Thinking: plan projects beyond a human lifetime
5. Holistic Forecasting: envision multiple pathways for civilization
6. Transcendent Goal: strive for one-planet thriving[35]

From these six, a curricular framework and learning objectives could be developed. Curriculum developers could easily draw on the many resources already available from the Long Now Foundation and The Long Time Project, plus other groups.

There will be the matter of competition for student time. Schools are routinely asked to take on new curricular tasks (usually without any consideration of what will be dropped in order to add in the new curriculum unit). So there will be the challenges of finding time in the school day to address the "time" curriculum. These are very real practical matters. There is always the possibility that a "time" curriculum will be developed, tried, and like many other curricular innovations, tossed aside, losing out in the ongoing competition for student time. (The other options, extending the school day or the school year or both, may seem reasonable in theory. But in practice, it seems unlikely that school districts or taxpayers will seriously consider such options.)

There is always the possibility that a "time" curriculum would have little success. Nonetheless, the possibilities are there: schools are and will be a major venue for cultural change and thus political change. Schools can be a major source for long-term change of time perspective.

Although organizations and schools are important sources for change, there is a third source that is the most important of all: ourselves. The questions we need to confront are not organizational or educational curriculum questions. The questions we must ask ourselves are ethical—questions involving the basic kinds of choices we want to make.

Rosabeth Moss Kanter argues that "People take the long view when they feel a commitment to those who come after them. . . . They care about posterity—their children and other people's children—and therefore see the need for actions to benefit the distant future."[36]

In one of his BBC Futures programs, Richard Fisher notes that humans can mentally do what other animals cannot do: time travel. Humans can imagine what they're going to do. "But sadly," he concludes, they do not always have "the will or the motivation to escape the salience of the present."[37]

We can choose to have a short-term perspective. Or we can choose to have a long-term perspective. Although we might be inclined toward the short (for the reasons we have considered in this chapter), that inclination isn't inherent in human nature. We can choose the long term—if we want to. We have to choose one or the other. But with the necessity of choice, we are then on ethical ground. Time perspective involves ethics. We have an ethical obligation to choose our time perspective.

The third and most important source for possibly changing to the long term is ourselves. If we are to take on the complexities of shifting time orientation, the first order of business is to understand that we are talking about choice, about ethical questions, bearing on ourselves as well as others. And we must persuade others, when asking them to consider the need to shift to the long term, that for all of us these are ethical questions, questions that cannot be answered in technical terms but only in terms of what we think is ethically right.

As we consider our choices for time perspective, we also need to note that we must not forsake the present, the short term. If we want to get something done, we have to pay attention to the here and now. When considering what we want to do, we of course will want to keep an eye on the long term. But the short term can never be overlooked. As has been suggested in a somewhat different context, people do not run into mountains, but they do stumble over anthills. And if we want to get something done, there are the many quotidian details that need attention. The immediate matters. Let's say we are in a town being threatened with flooding from spring melt. If the mayor dithers and wants to convene a citizens' advisory committee to consider all possible alternatives and all the long-term implications of those alternatives, we will override the mayor and get on with getting all the sandbags we can right now.

We need both the short term and the long term. We need, in effect, double vision, a kind of mixed scanning, considering the important details of the here and now, considering those details in view of the long term, and at the same time considering the very long term. A tall order, but that is the only way we are likely to secure and sustain a free society.

NOTES

1. "The Popularity of 'Time' Unveiled," *BBC News*, June 22, 2006, news.bbc.co.uk/2/hi/uk_news/5104778stm.
2. Marc Wittman, *Felt Time: The Science of How We Experience Time*, trans. Eric Butler (Cambridge: MIT Press, 2017).
3. Alexis de Tocqueville. *Democracy in America*, trans. Harvey Mansfield and Delba Winthrop (Chicago: University of Chicago Press, 2000), 512.
4. Kevin Kelly, "The Next 100 Years of Science: Long-Term Trends in the Scientific Method," The Long Now Foundation, Seminars about Long-Term Thinking, filmed March 10, 2006, http://longnow.org/seminars/02006/mar/10/long-term-trends-in-the-scientific-method.
5. Judy Wacjman, *Pressed for Time: The Acceleration of Time in Digital Capitalism* (Chicago: University of Chicago Press, 2015), and Robert Hassan, *Empires of Speed: Time and the Acceleration of Politics and Society* (Boston: Brill, 2009).
6. William Wordsworth, "The World Is Too Much with Us," https://poetryfoundation.org/poems/45564/the-world-is-too-much-with-us.
7. Ashley Whillans, *Time Smart: How to Reclaim Your Time and Live a Happier Life* (Cambridge: Harvard Business Review Press, 2020).
8. Carl Honoré, *In Praise of Slowness: Challenging the Culture of Speed* (San Francisco: HarperSanFrancisco, 2004).
9. Dominic Barton, "Capitalism for the Long Term," *Harvard Business Review* 89, no. 3 (March 2011): 84–91.
10. Dominic Barton, "Refocusing Capitalism on the Long Term," *Oxford Review of Economic Policy* 33, no. 2 (Summer 2017): 188–210.
11. John R. Graham, Campbell R. Harvey, and Shiva Rajgopal, "Value Destruction and Financial Reporting Decision," *Financial Analysts Journal* 62, no. 6 (Nov.-Dec. 2006): 27–39.
12. Alana Semuels, "How to Stop Short-Term Thinking at America's Companies," *The Atlantic*, December 30, 2016, https://www.theatlantic.com/bus/archive/2016/12/short-term-thinking/511874/.
13. "The Atlanta Public Schools Cheating Scandal," Georgia Public Policy Foundation, https://www.georgiapolicy.org/issue/the-atlanta-public-schools-cheating-scandal/.
14. Sean Blanda, "The Jeff Bezos School of Long-Term Thinking," March 2, 2013, https://www.seanblanda.com/the-jeff-bezos-school-of-long-term-thinking/.
15. Barton, "Capitalism for the Long Term," 84–91.

16. Vince Martin, "Short-Termism Isn't the Boogeyman You Think It Is," November 12, 2019, https://investorplace.com/2019/myth-short-termism-corporate-myopia-academic/.

17. See FCLTGlobal, https://www.fcltglobal.org.

18. For American Prosperity Project, see https://www.aspeninstitute.org/programs/business-and-society-program/american-prosperity-project/.

19. Sheldon S. Wolin, "What Time Is It?" *Theory and Event* 1, no. 1 (1997): 1–5.

20. Oxford Martin Commission for Future Generations, "Now for the Long Term: The Report of the Oxford Martin Commission for Future Generations," October 2013, https://www.oxfordmartin.ox.ac.uk/downloads/commission/Oxford_Martin_Now_for_the_Long_Term.pdf, 45.

21. Tocqueville, *Democracy in America*, 663.

22. Stewart Brand, *The Clock of the Long Now: Time and Responsibility* (New York: Basic Books, 1999), 157.

23. Abraham Flexner, *Medical Education in the United States and Canada* (New York: Arno Press, 1972). See also Charles Vevier, ed., *Flexner: 75 Years Later: A Current Commentary on Medical Education* (Lanham, M.D.: University Press of America, 1987).

24. Brand, *Clock of the Long Now*, 139.

25. Mancur Olson, "Dictatorship, Democracy, and Development," *The American Political Science Review* 87, no. 3 (September 1993): 567–76.

26. Robert Dallek, *Flawed Giant: Lyndon Johnson and His Times, 1961–1973* (New York: Oxford University Press, 1998), 190.

27. Quoted in Richard Fisher, "The Perils of Short-Termism: Civilization's Greatest Threat," *BBC*, January 9, 2019, https://www.bbc.com/future/article/20190109-the-perils-of-short-termism-civilisations-greatest-threat.

28. Ralph Lerner, *The Thinking Revolutionary: Principle and Practice in the New Republic* (Ithaca: Cornell University Press, 1987), 61.

29. Gregory Bateson, *Steps to an Ecology of Mind* (New York: Ballantine, 1972; reissued with a foreword by Mary Catherine Bateson, Chicago: University of Chicago Press, 2000), 492.

30. The Long Now Foundation, https://longnow.org.

31. Beatrice Pembroke and Ella Saltmarshe, "The Long Time," The Long Time Project, October 28, 2019, https://medium.com/@thelongtimeinquiry/the-long-time-3383b43d42ab.

32. Stewart Patrick, "Looking Past the Inbox: Report of the Oxford Martin Commission for Future Generations," Council on Foreign Relations, November 6, 2013, https://www.cfr.org/blog/looking-past-inbox-report-oxford-martin-commission-future-generations.

33. Graham Smith, "Why We Need a Committee for Future Generations in the House of Lords," Constitution Unit Blog, June 5, 2018, https://constitution-unit.com/tag/oxford-martin-commission-for-future-generations/.

34. Linda Gessner, "Knesset Commission for Future Generations," Foundation for Democracy & Sustainable Development, June 25, 2017, https://www.fdsd.org//?s=Knesset.

35. Roman Krznaric, "Six Ways to Think Long-Term: A Cognitive Toolkit for Good Ancestors," Long Now Foundation, July 20, 2020, https://medium.com/the-long-now-foundation/six-ways-to-think-long-term-da373b3377a4.

36. Rosabeth Moss Kanter, *On the Frontiers of Management* (Cambridge: Harvard University Press, 1997), 281.

37. Fisher, "The Perils of Short-Termism."

Chapter 3

Leadership in and for a Free Society

Leadership is a large topic. Any search on the website of any large research university library will yield at least two million entries, at least 49,000 books alone, plus hundreds of thousands of journal articles. With such a popular and complex topic, the most one can do, of course, is to treat a small portion of the whole. The small portion considered here pertains to leadership in and for a free society.

To speak of leadership in the context of a free society clearly claims that there is another kind of leadership, to wit, leadership in a non-free society, and that there are differences between the two. After an initial brief discussion of differences, we will move forward to our main task—identification of the ideal behaviors and attributes supportive of a free society, along with a consideration of how these behaviors and attributes might be realized.

Prior to moving along, it will be helpful to clarify how we might refer to various kinds of leaders. For our purposes here, to speak of leaders in non-free societies is to refer to all leaders, public and private, with no distinction made between "good" and "bad" leaders. As a matter of convenience, we can refer to them simply as "non-free leaders."

For public and private leaders in a free society, we will make a further distinction. There are two kinds of leaders in a free society. Some leaders are alert to the demands of a free society and behave accordingly to support the free society. Where useful, we will refer to these kinds of leaders as supportive free leaders. But there are other leaders who are not alert to the demands of a free society; these leaders tend to behave in non-supportive ways. Where useful, we will refer to them as non-supportive free leaders. As will be discussed below, there usually is some blending of the two: any given leader can (and often does) behave in both supportive and non-supportive ways. The desired behaviors and attributes can be postulated as ideals to be worked toward but not always to be achieved in full.

With these terms as specified, we can proceed to our first task—a consideration of differences between leadership in free and non-free societies. There are many ways to consider differences in leadership. The various differences, though, can be brought together under one fundamental rubric: whether leaders—all of us, actually—view people as means to the leaders' ends or whether we choose to view people as autonomous, free, and worthy as people not as means, but ends in themselves.

Law and English professor James Boyd White puts the fundamental rubric this way: "There is no sure-fire method of attaining your ends when those ends require the cooperation of others and that to recognize the freedom and autonomy of another, which is the only real possibility if one is to succeed at all, is necessarily to leave room for the exercise of that freedom and autonomy in ways you do not wish." White goes on to say that:

> All social action requires community and that community can never be compelled. . . . Our practical and moral lives are radically communal—unless perhaps we live alone on an island—and this means that our thought about what we want and who we are must reflect the freedom and power of others, without whose free cooperation we can have nothing of value, be nothing of value. This in turn means that hardheaded practical thought and sound ethical thought alike require us to recognize the existence of others and our dependence upon them. Our most practical end is never definable in terms of material results but always and only in terms of a certain kind of community: a way of facing the uncertainties of life together.[1]

The several claims embedded in this fundamental rubric clearly raise many questions. We need to ask ourselves what we see as freedom. What is autonomy? If community cannot be compelled, and community is seen as necessary, then how is community to be attained? What does it mean in practice to be dependent on others? And the several claims ask us to consider further the kinds of responses we can expect from people and especially from leaders in free and non-free societies.

A leader in a non-free society will regard the cooperation/community/autonomy rubric as nonsense, dangerous nonsense. The people immediately around you are there to do what you want them to do. You want to have your close associates go along with you and not try to have you killed. So you pay attention to them in order to make sure they are doing what you want and are not plotting against you. As for the great mass of people in his or her domain, the leader simply demands unquestioning compliance and hard work toward accomplishing the leader's goals. The non-free leader surely will reject the claim that it is necessary or desirable to "leave room for exercise of freedom and autonomy in ways you do not wish."

What the non-free leader rejects in this way of viewing people, supportive free leaders embrace. Supportive leaders in a free society will regard the fundamental rubric of community and cooperation and autonomy as the basis of their leadership behavior. Such leaders will recognize that rightness of White's assertion: community is necessary, and community simply cannot be compelled. At most, with attempts at compulsion, people will respond with superficial acquiescence—and underlying resentment.

The supportive free society leader will recognize that under all circumstances, people may adopt ideas or approaches of the leader, but they will always create their own interpretations of what the leader wants, and even while fully supporting the leader's demands or requests, people will necessarily constitute that support in whatever way they wish.

As we will see below in considering more specifically desired attributes and behaviors of leaders in a free society, there are many challenges to be met and temptations to be foresworn if one is to be a good leader. Non-free leaders in non-free societies will foreswear any authentic involvement with people other than in instrumental means–ends terms. But even in a free society, leaders are often tempted to disregard the legitimate concerns of citizens and see citizens only as means to an end.

Many free society leaders pay attention to other people only in terms of compliance, checking to make sure the message is getting across to the troops and making sure the message is being obeyed. There is nothing to suggest that in a free society leaders are inevitably drawn to the rubric of community, cooperation, and autonomy. Just because one is a leader in the context of a free society does not guarantee that the leader will act in accord with what a free society needs from leaders.

Only in a free society is there the possibility that a leader in that society can actually behave in ways properly supporting the free society. The only guarantee a free society offers to leaders is the opportunity to choose to behave in supportive ways or non-supportive ways. The leaders in a free society must choose. They must choose attributes, and they must choose how to behave. There is no option to *not* choose. Leaders, as with all of us, behave in one way or another. And in making choices, leaders, as with all of us, are on ethical ground.

As has long been argued, there must be choice for a matter to be considered ethical or unethical. If there is no choice in an action, the action is not in the ethical realm. One's height is not an ethical matter, because there is no opportunity to choose height. But if there is choice, then the matter is indeed ethical. How leaders choose to behave may be seen as a political choice, also as a cultural choice. But the ultimate grounding is ethical.

Not all choices have ethical implications, even if the choices are voluntary. Deciding between vanilla and chocolate ice cream isn't an ethical matter.

Other choices are. John Dewey helps makes the distinction: "Choice would hardly be significant if it did not take effect in outward action, and if it did not when expressed in deeds make a difference in things."[2] Surely, the choices leaders, and would-be leaders, make in deciding which attributes to acquire and which behaviors to exhibit make significant differences in securing and sustaining a free society.

ATTRIBUTES

It is to those attributes and behaviors of leaders in a free society that we now turn. We first examine two attributes: grounded identity and acceptance of a long-term time orientation. This discussion will be followed by a consideration of leadership behaviors that are related to reinforcing the critical elements of a free society.

NEED FOR GROUNDED IDENTITY

A critical attribute for supportive free leaders is a grounded identity: both a strong sense of self-identity and a sense of identity in relation to others. The view of the world proffered here is a particular view of community, cooperation, and autonomy, of uncertainty—a view that necessarily involves a lot of ambiguity and uncertainty. It is a view of not necessarily knowing what others are going to do, of give and take, and patience, and willingness to accept other people making meanings in ways that suit them. Above all, this fundamental view suggests the need to forsake the desire to control people and events. In order to be able to engage effectively and ethically in a world with this view deeply in mind, you have to know who you are both in terms of self-identity and identity in relation to others.

Organizational theorist James March suggests that Don Quixote gives us useful insight into the notion of self-identity.[3] Despite his tilting at windmills, the good knight can be seen as grounded in a very fundamental sense, as indicated by his insistent utterance, "yo sé quien soy," I know who I am and I do what I do because that is who I am. In this sense, behavior is not determined by consequences, as seen by the following example. You ride the bus every morning. Every time you board, you greet the driver. It's just something you do, part of who you are. Most drivers greet you in return. But if a driver doesn't greet you in return, that will not modify your behavior: you'll continue to greet that driver and all drivers.

At the same time, my sense of identity is developed in relation to others. I am not totally autonomous. I am aware that others are aware of me, reacting to me, assessing me. I interact with others and through that interaction I am continually shaping a sense of who I am or might be, some sort of social identity.[4] There is likely some tension, modest or more, between my sense of self-identity and my social identity—a tension that I need to be aware of, and make use of.

In developing both self-identity and identity in relation to others, it is necessary to be thoroughly honest. If we are not honest, we are creating a fantasy world hardly conducive to a healthy free society. In *The Brothers Karamazov*, Father Zosima gives profound advice to Fyodor Karamazov: "Do not lie to yourself. A man who lies to himself and listens to his own lie comes to a point where he does not discern any truth in himself and anywhere around him, and thus falls into disrespect towards himself and others."[5]

It is a difficult task, seeing ourselves clearly and understanding others clearly. We can convince ourselves that we need things that we really don't need. And sometimes we have needs that we refuse to acknowledge as needs. If we are unable to see our own needs with clarity, how much more difficult it is, then, to listen to and understand the needs of others.[6]

It is tempting to be dishonest, to lie to ourselves. We are tempted in the same way Chekhov says, quoting his fellow Russian writer Pushkin: "Dearer to us than a host of base truths is the illusion that exalts."[7]

Identity—self and social—involves choice. The only grounded way to choose and act on one's identity is to make the choice yourself. Either you choose your own identity or you allow others to define you. It is possible to let others define you, create your sense of who you are, but then we are on dangerous ground, not with "I know who I am," but "I am what you think I am."

Leaders in free societies should not think that recognizing "freedom and autonomy in ways you do not wish" means being a compliant lapdog, just doing whatever the people (whomever they are) tell you to do. The caution about lapdogs is warranted. There are plenty of lapdogs to be seen, especially around election time. There are some who seem to hop from one lap to another, and any lap will do. John Kennedy's *Profiles in Courage* highlighted the rare courageous leader, the leader who was not a lapdog. Perhaps the exceptions proved the rule: most politicians play it safe because they don't want to offend what they think is their "base."

It must be noted that a grounded sense of identity is no guarantee of goodness and a free society. Any dictator has a strong sense of identity. Stalin surely knew who he was and what he was about as he calmly went about the murder of millions of people.[8] Rather, the grounded sense of identity that we are saying is necessary for a free society is an identity in relation to others that recognizes others as human beings as ends in themselves, free and autonomous.

For the supportive free leader, then, a good grounded identity means being neither dictator nor lapdog. There are many complexities here. Again, James Boyd White provides a useful insight in commenting on the behavior of Odysseus in the Greek tragedy, *Philoctetes*: "Odysseus seems wholly unaware that who he is today has, or can have, any relation to who he will be tomorrow, or was yesterday. For him the self has no continuity but is a series of discrete and unconnected actions and moments of consciousness, a set of fragments. This means that rational thought about, and action in, the social and cultural realm is impossible."[9]

It is a complex matter, finding and acting on grounded identity. It is, however, a matter having direct bearing on a free society. If you don't know who you are and how to find yourself, you will be in no good position to do good by a free society and may find yourself doing it harm.

WILLINGNESS TO EMBRACE LONG-TERM TIME PERSPECTIVE

It is easy to give into a short-term time perspective. As shown in the previous chapter, the short term is everywhere, so common that we pay it little mind, other than to note that there is never enough to do what we want. Leaders and especially elected officials habitually attend to the prejudices of their base and not wanting to lose that base support fall into the rhythms of the short term very easily. To go against those rhythms, to push for another tempo, a slower tempo, is a daunting task, as can be seen by the several organizational advocacy efforts made to effect long-term time perspective. Those efforts, as we have seen, are extensive and ongoing. Were it easy to change a societal time perspective, it would already have been done.

Organizational advocacy efforts must continue. But in the short term, we must look to individual leadership, public and private, to actually accept long-term perspectives as a basic part of their leadership grounding. It may seem as if we are in a chicken-and-egg quandary. A politician runs for office every few years and feels the need to trumpet a list of accomplishments to show that he or she has responded to the desires of the constituency for immediate results or that he or she has voted to spend more now or tax less now and hope that Santa Claus will somehow make things right with far-off generations who will be paying for our short-term splurges. "You said it—you said give us the goodies right now, and let future generations deal with it, and that's what I have done, so re-elect me and we'll do more of the same."

This view of the politicians puts all of the responsibility on the constituency, the people out there, and all of the stimulus for any possible change. That the people have some responsibility here is clear enough, as we will continue to see in chapter 4. But to lay all of the responsibility at the door of the people is to indeed reduce leaders to lapdogs mindlessly doing the bidding of their owners.

This view does suggest that the people in their own way are also mindless, caught up in their own version of short-term bread and circuses, living for the moment and willing to damn future generations to penury to pay for current greed. We are left, then, with lapdog leaders and nonthinking selfish constituents.

A low estimate of both, and for the sake of the health of a free society, we have to reject that low estimate and entertain the possibility that we can do better. Leaders will have to go against the conventional wisdom. They will have to talk with (not at) constituencies about the long-term effects of the short-term fixation. Leaders must approach people with higher expectations in mind. "What kind of a people do they think we are?" Winston Churchill famously challenged in his address to a joint session of Congress in early 1942. Leaders must ask the same question of their constituencies, already having in view the possibility that people can rise, can do better.

What is suggested here is an approach similar to that taken by Abraham Lincoln in speaking with his constituency. Ralph Lerner argues that Lincoln was faced with a dilemma. He needs to nudge people from their self-satisfaction to a better way of viewing themselves and the world. If he chides the people, the people likely will pay him no mind. But if he flatters them, supports their mistaken beliefs, they will perhaps listen, but only to reinforce their mistaken beliefs and make matters worse. Lerner argues that Lincoln works things in a different way. Lincoln takes the people into his confidence, asking them to join him in looking at how they might view the world, at who they are and what they might become. From the outset, Lincoln knew that the "'great high road' to a man's reason has to be gained, not assumed or commanded or despised." As Lincoln observed, "I take it that I have to address an intelligent and reading community."[10]

Present day leaders would do well to follow Lincoln's approach. Assume the people are intelligent, thoughtful, willing to consider their situation. Ask more of the people. Remind the people of what and who they are. In commenting on Winston Churchill's approach to the people during World War II, historian Max Hastings observes that "From the outset, while he always insisted that victory would come, his personal prestige rested upon the honesty with which he acknowledged to the British people the gravity of the ordeal they faced."[11]

Perhaps we can say that Churchill, like Lincoln, had a sense of the British people as an intelligent and reading community. The British people had long had a tradition of autodidactic learning. The great majority of working class people belonged to at least one mutual improvement society. Throughout the eighteenth and into the nineteenth centuries, British people had established reading rooms, lending libraries, theater groups, musical groups, and more, all on a voluntary basis without benefit of government or clergy.[12] Churchill, as historian and politician, knew his answer to his own question about the nature of the British people. He did not underestimate the people, he did not disdain them.

To follow the approach of Lincoln or Churchill, leaders themselves must first be grounded in the long term while never losing sight of what needs to be taken care of in the short term. They must have an unwillingness to be forced into short-term expediences, tempting as these may be. They must look to the long term and judge proposed policies and actions accordingly. Moreover, with the possession of these attributes, leaders will be in a better position to remind people of the importance of the long term for securing and sustaining a free society.

BEHAVIORS

Many of the behaviors of leaders in free societies can be considered in terms of the necessary elements of a free society as outlined in chapter 1. In what follows, we discuss leadership behaviors in terms of four elements: (1) the ethics of persuasion, (2) the need for stable meaning of words and facts, (3) the ecology of persuasion, and (4) trust and social capital.

PERSUASION AND THE ETHICS OF PERSUASION

All leaders in all societies engage in persuasion, in trying to convince others to believe or act in desired ways. There are all sorts of ways to persuade. One can appeal to logic and facts, or to emotions, or to believe in the character of the persuader. One can use bribery: if you will do as I want, I'll give you money. One can engage in quid pro quo: I'll give you something you want, you give me something I want, and we're both happy. Or, one can go even further, perhaps beyond persuasion proper, and use or threaten to use force. Force is not persuasion. Force is evidence of a failure to persuade. As James Boyd White observes, "When persuasion fails, the boundaries of the culture are defined."[13]

A leader's choice of how to persuade says a great deal about the leader and what the leader thinks of the intended audience. What kind of world do you claim and constitute when you choose a given way of persuading? What kind of character do you define for yourself and offer to others when you choose to talk one way rather than another? And what kind of character do you attribute your audience when you talk one way rather than another? For example, if you suggest to your staff that blackmail would be a good way of persuading or at least neutralizing a political opponent, you are stating that you think blackmail is acceptable behavior to you and you calculate that your staff will also find blackmail acceptable.

There is always more than one way to persuade, more than one kind of grounding for an argument. There are choices to be made, and as we have noted earlier, if something is a matter of choice, then we are on ethical ground. A major ethical choice for any leader in a free society in considering approaches to persuasion bears on the distinction between a persuaded audience and a more thoughtful public.

Leaders, of course, want to persuade, and they look to create a persuaded audience. But, as noted in chapter 1, there are significant differences between a persuaded audience and something else—a more thoughtful public. All that is required for a persuaded audience is a group of people who agree with a leader. A lynch mob can be a persuaded audience, simply a group of people somehow persuaded to do evil. Sadly enough, the need for the Biblical commandment, "thou shalt not follow a multitude to do evil" tells us that such mobs have always been with us.

In a non-free society there are always attempts at persuasion. A persuaded audience is all that is required—a group of people complying with the leader's demands. The alternative, a more thoughtful public, with its questioning and skepticism, is not only not required, but it is always seen by the authorities as a kind of enemy action.

Persuasion in a non-free society is not automatic. Non-free leaders do pay attention to the politics and demands of persuasion. Faced with the June 1941 Nazi invasion, Stalin had to promote his people's support for the conflict by calling it the "Great Patriotic War." Stalin, a realist, suspected that people weren't going to fight to defend the Bolshevik tyranny, and in the course of the war, Stalin conceded that "they are fighting for the homeland, not for us."[14] That kind of persuasion was backed by an ominous threat: The Red Army command issued an edict to all armed forces: "Everyone who has been captured is a traitor to the Motherland," and most of the soldiers who managed to evade the Nazis and make it back home were either imprisoned or executed.[15]

But in a free society, a leader must go beyond wanting a persuaded audience: the leader must have a more thoughtful public in mind. Rather than being just a passive audience, a recipient of whatever the leader is trying to persuade about, a thoughtful public interacts with the leader, pushes back, is critical, skeptical, demanding of proof. The purpose of persuasion is not to impose but to engage. The good leader in a free society will always have a thoughtful public in mind, not as something to be opposed and overcome, but something to be encouraged and developed.

As always, there are no guarantees. A more thoughtful public is not a plebiscitary democracy. Just as a leader isn't necessarily right, a bunch of people, a crowd, a public isn't necessarily right. We can certainly be skeptical about the rightness of "top-down" perspectives. But there is equally no warrant to uncritically accept what comes from "bottom-up" perspectives.

WORDS AND FACTS: THE NEED FOR STABLE MEANING

Part of persuasion in a more thoughtful public involves people weighing and considering, talking with leaders and with each other. In order to weigh and consider thoughtfully, in order to have intelligent and rational discourse, words have to have stable, agreed-upon meaning, and there must be respect for facts. As philosopher Richard Weaver put it, "community rests upon informed sentiment."[16]

Words have to have meaning, stable meaning commonly accepted. In *Standing by Words*, Wendell Berry specifies three conditions for a meaningful statement: "It must designate its object precisely"; "its speaker must be willing to stand by it; must believe it, be accountable for it, be willing to act on it"; and "this relation of speaker, word, and object must be conventional: the community must know what it is."[17] We cannot accept a world in which words mean whatever someone says they mean at the time. Humpty Dumpty may so claim that for words, but we must say no.

Rulers who wish to disguise their intentions and actions encourage language in which words have no meaning. As George Orwell put it in one of his most celebrated essays: "The great enemy of clear language is insincerity. When there is a gap between one's real and one's declared aims, one turns as it were instinctively to long words and exhausted idioms. . . . When the general atmosphere is bad, language must suffer."[18] Orwell's observations are echoed by Romanian novelist Mikhail Sebastian: "Words are losing their meaning. . . . Their speakers do not believe them, while their hearers do not understand them." If you compared declarations in the daily newspapers to the facts to which they refer, Sebastian said, "You would see that there is an absolute split between word and reality."[19]

There must be respect for facts, facts that are in accord with the real world as we commonly know it. A telling part of Orwell's *1984*: Winston Smith, under torture is asked to agree that two plus two equals five if that is what Big Brother says it equals. No, Winston says, it's four. Let's try again, says his torturer. And at long last, Winston says that two plus two equals five. As reflected in this horrifying sequence, Orwell knew the great importance of facts and what happens in a society when facts, like words, no longer have commonly ascribed meaning, but are facts only as defined by ruling powers.

In a free society, facts must be acknowledged as facts, however unpleasant the facts might be to some. For years, tobacco companies did all they could to deny the facts regarding the causal relationship between cigarette smoking and cancer. And in more recent years, we have seen blatant disregard for facts and the substitution of lies or "alternative facts" claimed as actual facts. Of the many thousands of lies promulgated by the Trump Administration, two seem particularly salient here.

President Trump and his press secretary claimed that the attendance at the presidential inauguration was the greatest in American history, while in fact, as shown by numerous overhead photographs, the crowd attending the Obama inauguration was much larger. And, shortly after the November 2020 presidential election, in bragging about the huge crowd that turned out to support Trump's claims of a stolen election, Press Secretary Kayleigh McEnany, claimed in a tweet that more than a "million" of the faithful had gathered, when in fact the number on the streets was at most about ten thousand.[20]

When the minister of information, echoed by Trump, can claim with a straight face and in the face of great ridicule and skepticism that a "million" is true while the actual reality is several thousand, a free society is surely threatened. It doesn't take torture to have people accept that two plus two equals five or that one million people were in a public square rather than several thousand; all it takes are leaders and people who no longer think that truth matters.

People in a free society, a more thoughtful public, need to have access to the facts, as much access as possible within necessary bounds of privacy and personnel laws (and, where necessary, national security). They must have access to facts if they are going to weigh and consider and get at what is true, what is probable, what is false.

The importance of the availability of information can be seen by the extraordinary efforts always taken in non-free societies to ensure that people are deprived of facts and information, and the extraordinary efforts made to substitute whatever sets of facts the non-free society rulers think is appropriate. As a general rule, when there is a revolution, a coup, a forceful takeover of any kind in a regime, one of the first actions of the newly emerging regime is to seize control of all communications facilities—newspapers, radios, television, and in recent years, social media.

And, once established, non-free rulers do what is necessary to solidify the control of information flow. The Great Firewall in the People's Republic of China is but one example of this kind of control. The control isn't always totally successful. The Great Firewall is seen by many in China as a challenge, something to be hacked. The attempt and the responses are reminiscent of the observation in the *Tao Te Ching* 58 that in countries ruled with severity, the people respond with cunning.

In contrast, a good leader in a free society has an obligation to words and to facts, to transparency. The good leader will insist on clear language, on avoiding euphemisms, on telling the truth. The good leader will not lie. And the good leader will ensure that the facts are available, not just in response to newspapers suing under freedom-of-information acts, but actively and affirmatively making efforts to provide to all people as much as can be provided. It was noted just above that there are circumstances under which facts cannot be provided to the public.

Many of these prohibitions have reasonable grounding, for example, personnel matters or attorney-client privilege. A common claimed grounding is, as noted, national security. This grounding can be reasonable but can also be used to cover up much that arguably should be open to all. The good leader in a free society will insist on clear justification from administrative staff when reviewing what is kept secret and conduct that kind of review on a regular basis.

THE ECOLOGY OF PERSUASION

There is an ethics of persuasion, ways of choosing how to try to persuade others. We can also consider persuasion in an ecological sense. Just as there is an ecology of things in the world, there is an ecology of ideas. Ideas are connected, and they influence each other. As Gregory Bateson concludes, in his *Steps to an Ecology of Mind*, "The means by which one man influences another are part of the ecology of ideas in their relationship, and part of the larger ecological system within which that relationship exists."[21]

A choice to talk a certain way, use a certain kind of argument, may very well have an impact on how other people will be inclined to argue. For example, art teachers in a school district, concerned about lack of support for the arts, might choose to claim that there was research showing that students who took art classes did significantly better on statewide standardized achievement tests than students who didn't take art. Art leads to higher test scores is a choice of argument. The art teachers could have chosen another argument, namely, art is a part of what it means to be human, and all students—everyone—should have the opportunity to better understand and appreciate art, irrespective of test scores. Each argument incorporates a view of art in relation to the world; the former is consequential: art is valued as long as it leads to higher test scores; the latter is normative: art is worthy in and of itself.

If the art teachers are successful with their test scores argument, and the school board and administration go ahead with greatly increased support for the arts, the lesson will not be lost on other groups of teachers concerned about support for their programs. The music teachers, watching their colleagues in the arts, will very well likely say to themselves, "We think music is important to everyone because music is part of the human condition, but look at what the art teachers did—they talked to the school board in terms of test score payoff, and it worked, so maybe that's the kind of argument we should use, too. We'll somehow try to show that music is valuable because it leads to higher test scores." Some music teachers might say that that kind of argument makes them uncomfortable. Music is music, it's not just some way to crank up test scores. But other music teachers, on the pragmatic side, will reply, "The test score argument worked for our friends in the art department, that's what seemed to convince the school board."

We can multiply this example across school districts. Art teachers belong to national professional associations. So do music teachers. The "success" of the art teachers in one school district in one part of the country becomes known, not just locally but throughout the country, among art teachers and among music teachers.

The choice of how one wishes to argue, then, is an ecological choice: the basis of one's argument will not only affect your own immediate domain, it stands a good chance to affect the domain of others. Our example here deals with art and music teachers. The ecology of persuasion and the choices involved pertain just as much to the conduct of politics and political campaigns.

For example, in the aftermath of the November 2020 gubernatorial campaign in Washington State, the Republican candidate announced that he was not going to concede and would never concede that his Democratic opponent had legitimately won. Just as there are copycat crimes, there are copycat political strategies, part of the ecology: what one candidate does at the national level will be picked up at other levels. The Republican candidate for governor and his campaign manager claimed massive fraud at the polls, despite what election officials (also Republican) said were "unsubstantiated claims" and "no tangible evidence of irregularities." Undeterred by an election in which he secured all of 43 percent of the statewide vote, losing by more than 545,000 votes, the Republican candidate says he will press on, go to court, sue, and ask for donations to fund the effort to delegitimize the election.[22]

More commonly, the kinds of persuasion found in political campaigns are down and dirty attacks, lies, photoshopping, and social media lies—hardly conducive to securing and sustaining a more thoughtful public in a free society.

The good leader in a free society has an obligation to counter the gutter rhetoric, the attack ads, the lies. Some politicians make modest attempts at countering. One sometimes hears a politician say, "I will not run dirty attack ads; I will not run a negative campaign." But there usually is a proviso: "However, if my opponent persists in peddling lies about me, I will of course have no choice but to reply and counterattack." And off we go. Other politicians are aware that negative campaigns have a downside and are hardly inspiring. But, some politicians will say, "they work."

They work, it is said, because that is what the people want. Perhaps that is what some might say the people want. Again, though, we can hearken back to Lincoln and his approach, his wanting to assume a thoughtful public. In response to people wanting to hear negativity and attacks and lies, the good leader in a free society, the good politician will say: "I won't allow you to let me talk that way."

As Richard Weaver reminds us, there is no utterance without responsibility and consequence. However leaders wish to talk is connected to others and how they will talk. A leader has to choose, but one of the choices never available is avoiding choice. If you want people to be thoughtful and reflective, speak in thoughtful and reflective ways. If you want something else, you'll get something else.

ENCOURAGING TRUST AND SOCIAL CAPITAL

Trust, social capital, and being a more thoughtful public are critical elements of a free society. Leaders are always in a position to either support or ignore or do damage to all three of these elements. A leader who habitually lies or otherwise reinforces disrespect for expertise and plain facts (through supporting fantasized "alternative" facts) will destroy the trust relationship between the leader and many citizens. Moreover, by promulgating lies and disregarding truth, leaders in effect provoke citizens not to trust science, expertise, or each other.

Much is to be gained when there is trust—thoughtful trust. An example of trust contributing to effective response to a civic problem can be seen in the strategies developed in response to a severe drought in Seattle some years ago. The drought caused a water shortage. Water engineers said that unless people refrained from watering their lawns during the summer months, no water at all would be available some months later. The mayor and city council concurred, adopting a resolution prohibiting lawn watering for several months.

The prohibition was followed: people did not water their lawns during the specified time period. The crisis was dealt with, in large part because of the high level of trust between citizens, the water engineers, the mayor, and the city council. The trust, it should be noted, was not "blind." Hearings were held, citizens were able to critically examine the data provided by engineers to the mayor and city council; all officials involved were available for as much time as people had questions.

Thinking further of the Seattle drought situation, we can imagine what might have happened if the mayor had had a propensity to lie, to avoid facing facts. The mayor might have denied that there was a water shortage; the mayor might have attacked the water engineers as incompetent; the mayor might have attacked city council members as being in the thrall of the opposition party; the mayor might have encouraged citizens to disregard all of the drought data and instead just go ahead and water their lawns as much as they wanted to. If these had been the actions of the mayor, there would have indeed been a severe water shortage, and moreover, they would have encouraged a lack of trust among all parties. This lack of trust would have extended far beyond the water shortage issue and would have negatively tinctured city politics and operations in all areas.

Similarly, a leader can encourage or discourage the development and improvement of social capital. Developing social capital takes practice, and with practice, people get better. As noted in chapter 1, people can get together to work through a modest problem and, in the process of working together, discover that they have the ability and the potential to do more, whether it is a matter of dealing with potholes in neighborhood streets, lack of adequate street lighting, or increased crime in the neighborhood, and more.

A leader such as a city mayor can encourage social capital development through establishing as routine the involvement of all sorts of citizen groups in the development of policy in city governmental areas such as budget, police, housing, neighborhood business development, land use, pedestrian and bicycle lanes. For social capital development to actually occur, such citizen group involvement must be more than simply coming to meetings to hear what the mayor has to say: to be limited to sitting and hearing would reduce the citizen group to nothing more than a passive audience. Rather, the citizens must have an active role in exploring all aspects of whatever policy matter is under consideration.

Making authentic citizen involvement part of social capital development has serious implications for leaders. The process invites critical examination, close questioning, consideration and reconsideration, and active listening. As a result, the process inevitably takes time—time for people initially involved in the process to get to know and trust each other, time to consider and reconsider information, and time to consider and reconsider policy recommendations. Leaders must have a finely developed sense of a long-term time perspective combined with an awareness of short-term demands and practicalities. Part of that sense must include having a great deal of patience with others, and even oneself.

There are many aspects of leadership in and for a free society. We have considered some of those aspects, albeit briefly. Notions of identity, time frame, ethics and ecology of persuasion, the importance of words and facts, the need for trust and social capital: all of these merit careful consideration. There are other aspects of leadership that should not be overlooked, although not dealt with here.

Leaders need to reflect on and deal with all of the enabling conditions for a free society, as outlined in chapter 1. Moreover, leaders need to think about and act on their responsibilities for establishing and sustaining good schools for all. After all, nobody is born knowing what it takes to be a good citizen and what good citizens should expect of leaders in a free society. Issues of needed schooling will be discussed in greater detail in chapter 5.

These several aspects of leadership all bear on an overall critical variable: how a leader views people and their place in the world. As with the other aspects of leadership, how a leader views the basic nature of people is a matter of choice. Many leaders choose to see people in general as a flock of sheep, passive, in need of a good deal of guidance, not terribly bright.

Those who choose to view people in this way will resonate with Lonesome Rhodes, the demagogue television personality in Budd Schulberg's 1957 movie, *A Face in the Crowd*. Expressing his contempt for his television audience, he sneers, "Those morons out there? I toss 'em a dead fish and they flap their flippers. . . . I could make 'em eat dogfood and think it was steak."[23]

We have already noted the sentiments of Lord Protector Oliver Cromwell: "it's what the people need, not what they want." And, with this view of people, leaders will second what Stevens, the butler in *The Remains of the Day*, tells us: "A butler's duty is to provide good service. It is not to meddle in the great affairs of the nation. . . . Such great affairs will always be beyond the understanding of those such as you and I." Our duty, Stevens says, is "devoting our attention to those great gentlemen in whose hands the destiny of civilization truly lies."[24] On this view, the great mass of people not only do not know very much: more likely it is that they cannot know.

Even after the Bible had been legally published in English, Henry VIII tried to prohibit reading of Scripture, limiting reading and discussion of the Bible to graduates of Oxford and Cambridge Universities.[25] After all, once people started reading the Bible and making their own interpretations, who knows what they might do next. These are the dangers of education. And thus, two hundred years later, the same concerns were expressed. French lawyer Gourdin de'Arzac, for example, argued that any instruction "that tends, by cultivating a child's mind, to cause him to leave the place that nature has assigned him is always and absolutely as disadvantageous to him as it is harmful to the state, because it inverts the order of things."[26]

Perhaps the apotheosis of the argument for keeping people in their humble place—a place that people are actually happy with, unless disturbed by subversive education—is that famously stated by Dostoevsky's Grand Inquisitor: People don't want the burdens of freedom; they want nothing more than security; they want to be ruled by miracle, mystery, and authority. The people, in this view, are passive. They are, as Edmund Burke portrays them in *Reflections on the Revolution in France*, "thousands of great cattle, reposed beneath the shadows of the British oak, [who] chew the cud, and are silent."[27]

Leaders in and for free societies must reject this overarching view of people as sheep, as people unworthy of, indeed, incapable of, freedom. People do indeed want freedom. They are aware, and can become more aware, of the necessary tension between "freedom that is not license and the order that is not oppression."[28] People are capable, autonomous, thinking; they are surely capable of weighing and considering, and much more. We are back, then, to James Boyd White and his perspective outlined in the beginning of this chapter: we need to recognize the freedom and autonomy of others and recognize that without the "free cooperation of others" we will have nothing of value.

We must recognize that people are free individuals, capable of making conscious and responsible choices, and willing and able to take moral responsibility for their beliefs and actions. That, in broad terms, is the choice we must make. Those unsupportive of a free society will choose to believe that people are incapable of freedom. Those supportive of a free society will of course believe the opposite: that people are indeed capable of freedom. We cannot choose the option of not choosing.

We must recognize that not all current and would-be public and private leaders choose a free society. They may claim they support a free society, but they do not manifest the attributes and behaviors required by that society. As such, we must ask a critical question: Is it possible to increase the likelihood of getting the kinds of leaders we need and deserve?

Current and would-be leaders are capable of acquiring new attributes and altering behaviors in order to increase support of a free society. Change, although usually gradual in such matters, does happen. For example, many leaders have become more aware of and have acted on issues related to sexism. It has taken many decades of political effort and the work is hardly completed, but significant progress has been made in opportunities and working conditions for women. What would have been newsworthy several decades ago is now seen as commonplace, hardly worthy of notice. For example, for many years males comprised the great majority of enrollment in American medical schools. But, in the last thirty years, the enrollment has changed drastically: in many American medical schools the distribution of male and female students is roughly equal. The parity is now taken as a matter of course, not as something to be reported on the news. Leaders change, norms change, culture changes.

Part of the impetus for change comes from lawsuits or threats of lawsuits, or from protests, or from boycotts or threats of boycotts. But a large part of the impetus for change comes from changes in people's expectations—expectations of themselves, expectations they have of others, and expectations of leaders. It is to these expectations of citizens in and for a free society that we turn to in chapter4.

NOTES

1. James Boyd White, "Heracles' Bow: Persuasion and Community in Sophocles' *Philoctetes*," in *Heracles' Bow: Essays on the Rhetoric and the Poetics of the Law* (Madison: University of Wisconsin Press, 1985), 23, 25.

2. John Dewey, "Philosophies of Freedom," in *John Dewey: The Later Works, 1925–1953, vol. 3, 1927–1928*, ed. Jo Ann Boydston (Carbondale: Southern Illinois University Press, 1984), 104.

3. James March, "Yo sé quien soy," in *The Beat of a Different Drummer: Essays on Educational Renewal in Honor of John I. Goodlad*, eds. Kenneth A. Sirotnik and Roger Soder (New York: Peter Lang, 1999).

4. For still useful early consideration of self-identity, see Charles Horton Cooley, *Human Nature and the Social Order* (New York: Charles Scribner's Sons, 1902; New York: Taylor and Francis, 2017). See also George Herbert Mead, *Mind, Self, & Society*, ed. Charles W. Morris (Chicago: University of Chicago Press, 1934; 1962).

5. Fyodor Dostoevsky, *The Brothers Karamazov*, trans. Richard Pevear and Larissa Volokhonsky (San Francisco: North Point Press, 1990), 44.

6. Michael Ignatieff, *The Needs of Strangers: An Essay on Privacy, Solidarity, and the Politics of Being Human* (New York: Penguin Books, 1986), 11.

7. Anton Chekhov, *Stories*, trans. Richard Pevear and Larissa Volokhonsky (New York: Bantam, 2000), 465.

8. For comprehensive and careful critical examination of Stalin and mass murders, see Robert Conquest, *The Great Terror: A Reassessment* (New York: Oxford University Press, 1990); and Robert Conquest, *The Harvest of Sorrow: Soviet Collectivization and the Terror-Famine* (New York: Oxford University Press, 1986). See also Stéphane Courtois, Nicolas Werth, Jean-Louis Panné, Andrzej Paczkowski, Karel Bartošek, and Jean-Louis Margolin, *The Black Book of Communism: Crimes, Terror, Repression*, trans. Jonathan Murphy and Mark Kramer (Cambridge: Harvard University Press, 1999).

9. White, "Heracles' Bow," 21.

10. Ralph Lerner, *Revolutions Revisited: Two Faces of the Politics of Enlightenment* (Chapel Hill: University of North Carolina Press, 1994), 97.

11. Max Hastings, *Winston's War: Churchill, 1940–1945* (New York: Knopf, 2010), 61.

12. Jonathan Rose, *The Intellectual Life of the British Working Classes* (New Haven: Yale University Press, 2001).

13. James Boyd White, *When Words Lose Their Meaning: Constitutions and Reconstitutions of Language, Character, and Community* (Chicago: University of Chicago Press, 1984), 37.

14. Robert Conquest, *Stalin: Breaker of Nations* (New York: Viking, 1991), 239.

15. Conquest, *Stalin*, 293.

16. Richard Weaver, "Reflections of Modernity," in *Life without Prejudice, and Other Essays* (Chicago: Regnery, 1965), 118.

17. Wendell Berry, *Standing by Words* (San Francisco: North Point Press, 1983), 24.

18. George Orwell, "Politics and the English Language," in *The Collected Essays, Journalism and Letters of George Orwell*, eds. Sonia Orwell and Ian Angus (New York: Harcourt Brace Jovanovich, 1968), 4:137.

19. Mikhail Sebastian, *Journal 1935–1944: The Fascist Years*, trans. Patrick Camiller (Chicago: Ivan Dee, 2000), 334.

20. Mili Godio, "White House Press Secretary Kayleigh McEnany Wildly Exaggerates Trump March Crowd Size," *Newsweek*, November 14, 2020, https://www.newsweek.com/white-house-press-secretary-kayleigh-mcenany-wildly-exaggerates-trump-march-crowd-size-1547493.

21. Gregory Bateson, *Steps to an Ecology of Mind* (New York: Ballantine, 1972; reissued with a foreword by Mary Catherine Bateson, Chicago: University of Chicago Press, 2000), 492.

22. On the refusal of Washington State gubernatorial candidate to concede, see Jim Brunner, "Loren Culp, Refusing to Concede Washington Gubernatorial Race, Turns on Top Republicans," *Seattle Times*, November 21, 2020, https://www.seattletimes.com/seattle-news/politics/loren-culp-refusing-to-concede-washington-gubernatorial-race-turns-on-top-republicans/.

23. Budd Schulberg, *A Face in the Crowd* (New York: Ballantine, 1957), 142.

24. Kazuo Ishiguro, *The Remains of the Day* (New York: Vintage International, 1989), 199.

25. Rose, *Intellectual Life*, 13.

26. Quoted in Harvey Chisick, *The Limits of Reform in the Enlightenment: Attitudes toward the Education of the Lower Classes in Eighteenth-Century France* (Princeton: Princeton University Press, 1981), 173.

27. Edmund Burke, *Reflections on the Revolution in France* (Indianapolis: Bobbs-Merrill, 1957), 97.

28. Leo Strauss, *Persecution and the Art of Writing* (1952; Chicago: University of Chicago Press, 1988), 37.

Chapter 4

Citizens in and for a Free Society

We have considered the roles leaders might play in securing and sustaining a free society. But what of the people, the citizens, in and for a free society? What are their responsibilities to themselves and to others? What might best be their attributes, their behaviors? And how, in particular, are citizens to act in relation to those they have chosen as leaders?

As we begin to sort through these and related questions, it is important to remind ourselves of the critical difference between rulers and leaders. Ralph Lerner speaks of that difference in analyzing the American founding: "The new American Regime was no direct democracy, but neither was it designed for a people to be ruled by those who were their betters. Henceforth the people might be led, not ruled, and by leaders of their own choosing."[1]

Rulers, it can be said, rule *subjects*. Leaders lead *citizens*. In a non-free society, people are subjects whose modest and meek role is obeying their leaders. We cannot have a free society in which people are subjects whose only responsibility is to obey. For a society to be free, people must be citizens consenting to be led by those they have chosen.

A free society does not guarantee the goodness of leaders or citizens. Citizens can be poorly led or they can be led well. And citizens can allow themselves to be poorly led or they can allow themselves to be led well. There are choices to be made in what we as citizens allow. In a free society, citizens have to assume or ignore the responsibilities for what they allow.

The roles citizens play, the responsibilities they choose to assume or let pass by, derive from a complex cultural mix. Tocqueville once again is our guide: "I am quite convinced that political societies are not what their laws make them, but what sentiments, beliefs, ideas, habits of the heart, and the spirit of men who form them, prepare them in advance to be, as well as what nature and education have made them." The focus, Tocqueville argued, must be on "the sentiments, the ideas, the mores that alone can lead to public prosperity and liberty, what are the vices and errors that, on the other hand, divert them irresistibly from this."[2]

What kinds of attributes and behaviors of citizens—not subjects—can we reasonably ask for in seeking to secure and sustain a free society? What should be our expectations of ourselves, of others, and of those we choose to lead?

If we are, then, to secure and sustain a free society, what should be our expectations of ourselves, of others, and of those we choose to lead? What are the critical elements that we need to have in mind as we consider what it means to be citizens in and for a free society? In what follows, we turn to a discussion of four elements: (1) grounded identity, (2) tolerance for ambiguity, (3) deep appreciation for the requirements of freedom, and (4) need for long-term time frame.

This discussion is followed by a consideration of critical behaviors in and toward a more thoughtful public, including the art of active listening and the need for a careful view toward the past and the future. We conclude with a discussion of what citizens must expect of leaders in and for a free society.

GROUNDED IDENTITY

Maintaining a grounded identity is critical. If you don't know who you are, you will not be able to relate to others in authentic ways. As noted in chapter 3, we speak of identity in two ways: one's self-identity and one's social identity. Strong self-identity allows one to act without one's behavior being dependent on the behavior of others: you do what you do, because that is what you do. Social identity is developed and shaped in relation to others—what they think and believe and how they behave toward you.

As per chapter 3, it is critical to be thoroughly honest when developing social identity. It is perhaps important enough to risk tedious redundancy to repeat the wise admonition of Father Zosima: "Do not lie to yourself. A man who lies to himself and listens to his own lie comes to a point where he does not discern any truth in himself and anywhere around him, and thus falls into disrespect towards himself and others."[3]

It is not at all easy to be thoroughly honest. We know that for various reasons we sometimes are not thoroughly honest in our dealings with others. A friend shows you a newly purchased hat. Clearly pleased, the friend asks what you think. Even if you think the hat is unbecoming, you'll probably respond with less than thorough honesty, something along the lines of "if it works for you, great!" As Francis Bacon put it, "It asketh a strong wit and a strong heart to know when to tell truth, and to do it."[4]

It is perhaps even more difficult to be thoroughly honest with oneself. We can think we are being honest, objective, unafraid to look in the mirror and assess what we see. But we can easily go astray. Historian Edward Gibbon speaks of "how a wise man may deceive himself, how a good man can deceive others, how the conscience can slumber in a mixed and muddled state between self-illusion and voluntary fraud."[5]

In developing social identity, we are attuned to others. We are particularly attuned to others when developing those parts of our social identity dealing with politics and political activity. "Those parts" suggests multiple social identities. For many people, part—sometimes all—of social identity is developed in relation to ethnicity, gender, national origin, as well as movement politics and groups (environment, climate change, economic inequality, and the like). Social issues and politics can become viewed almost exclusively from the perspective of social identity, leading to various kinds of identity politics.

While identity politics—with its sharp focus on difference and on concerns of a particular group—can sometimes result in social and economic progress, identity politics can have a downside. Francis Fukuyama argues that "the shift in agendas of both left and right toward the protection of ever narrower group identities ultimately threatens the possibility of communication and collective action." Instead, he says, "we need to define larger and more integrative national identities that take account of the de facto diversity of existing liberal democratic societies."[6]

Fukuyama postulates six advantages of having strong national identity: (1) physical security and increased power to protect; (2) reduced corruption (because officials will keep resources from being diverted to their own ethnic group, political party, or other identity group); (3) increased economic development ("if people don't take pride in their country, they will not work on its behalf"); (4) trust developed on the widest possible radius rather than trust within various identity groups; (5) social safety nets that aid weaker people (rather than zero-sum competition between various self-regarding identity groups); and (6) greater hope for liberal democracy.[7]

Of this most important relationship between national identity and liberal democracy, Fukuyama argues that liberal democracy involves a trade: citizens give up some rights in order to have other rights protected (if you will, the tension between freedom and order). "National identity is built around the legitimacy of this contract; if citizens do not believe they are part of the same polity, the system will not function."[8]

Fukuyama goes further in his discussion of importance of national identity. "Democracies will not survive if citizens are not in some measure irrationally attached to the ideas of constitutional government and human equality through feelings of pride and patriotism. These attachments will see societies through their low points, when reason alone may counsel despair at the working of institutions."[9]

We can look to the British and their conduct during World War II to see a good example. "What kind of a people do they think we are?" asked Churchill in early 1942. The British people had already answered by their exemplary behavior during the worst of the 1940 bombings: a good people, attached with pride and patriotism to their government, their free society.[10]

Grounded identity, then, is critical to the healthy functioning of a free society. We must have a good self-identity, and we must have grounded multiple social identities. We must maintain our identity of who we are socially, economically, culturally, with all the diversity that those identities obtain, and at the same time, we must have a grounded national identity as part of what we hold in common. Maintaining an authentic balance here is challenging and necessary.

TOLERANCE FOR AMBIGUITY

Citizens in a free society have to deal in one way or another with all sorts of complex problems that admit of no easy solution, sometimes no solution at all. Many of the problems stem from the need to decide how to allocate scarce resources. There are never enough resources, and thus, as we have noted, the essential question in a free society—any society—is who is to get what and why.

The problems are complex because there are always many variables to consider. The complexity is increased given that there are no sets of problem-solving rules that can be applied with certainty to guarantee good solutions.

In order to understand some of the complexities of these problems and why it is too challenging to deal with them, we might first consider a simple hypothetical problem and why it poses little challenge. A person wants to go from point A to point B, three hundred miles away. The person drives a car at a constant speed of fifty miles per hour. How long will it take to get from A to B? The answer, the only answer, is obvious. It is a simple problem, with few variables and standard mathematical problem-solving rules.

But once we move from the hypothetical world to the actual world, the solving of the A to B driving time becomes much more of a challenge. We have many actual world variables that might intrude. The driver might or might not maintain a constant speed because of traffic congestion. Or road construction. Or bad weather. Or a flat tire. The driver might feel sick and have to stop for a bit. There might not be enough fuel to get all the way to point B. It may be that point B is under quarantine because of a widespread virus and our driver is stopped five miles before point B. With all these variables to consider—and the list here is hardly exhaustive—the problem is much more complex. The most we can do is calculate the probability of the time it will take to go from A to B. There is no one "right" answer. At most, we can think about an estimate, a range of time.

Our actual world problem can then become even more complex. We could make a wager with the driver: twenty dollars that the driver will take longer than X hours to make the trip. The driver agrees to the bet. Somewhere on the way, there is unexpected road construction, cars are halted for thirty minutes. Our driver considers going considerably over the speed limit in order to make up for lost time. As such, the problem takes on the added dimension of risk calculation: twenty dollars to be gained, but at the risk of getting a sixty dollar speeding ticket. It may be, even, in considering whether to make the wager in the first place, the driver will want to factor in the potential of delay and the risks involved if a delay does occur.

As we can see with this modest example, it doesn't take much for the simple to become very complex. And for citizens constantly facing problems in a free society, further complexities intrude. A hypothetical mathematical problem can be worked on and solved without worrying about other variables suddenly rearing up, throwing calculations off. But citizens are not isolates: they live in a free society that is subject to intrusion by many variables. Everything is in flux, everything is dynamic, everything is uncertain.

The free society can be seen as an open system existing in an environment in which the society imports information and resources from other parts of the environment and, by one means or another, exports something back to other parts.[11] We can for illustrative purposes consider a K-12 public school. The school is always interacting with other parts in its environment. The school imports supportive resources—levy money, support from businesses, PTA fundraisers. The school imports (enrolls) students. The school has to deal with myriad externally imposed rules and regulations.

The school functions in an environment where unpredictability is one of the few constants. Rules and regulations change. Every year some students leave, other students enter. Teachers and other staff members change. Central administrators and school boards change, and with those changes come different philosophies, different views of what the school should be doing.

As with our illustrative K-12 school, so too, all parts of a free society and all of its problems must be dealt with. The problems involve many interrelated variables, and the values of the variables are always changing, and the ways of approaching solutions are themselves uncertain and open to question.

For example, consider a problem we have already referred to: the necessary tension between freedom and order. There is no automatic answer here, no way to say with certainty just how much freedom versus just how much order. What is needed is for all of us to be talking with each other about how to frame the freedom–order tension. What we might conclude under the circumstances existing now might very well be different from what others conclude under differing circumstances one or five or ten years from now.

Given this context of uncertainty and unpredictability that pervades all aspects of a free society, the need for high tolerance for ambiguity becomes apparent.[12] Citizens must be comfortable with ambiguous problems and situations that admit of no quick answer, indeed, of no answer at all. Citizens must refuse to rush to judgment. Citizens must recognize that there is no decision-making situation in which everyone will have all the information deemed necessary to make a decision. Rather, citizens must be comfortable with, and adept with, the world of probabilities, of likelihood, of balanced risk assessment.

It is not easy to cultivate a tolerance for ambiguity. The rush to get on with things, the pressures of short time frames, the temptation to fall in with simplistic definitions of problems, and the belief that there are indeed "right" answers out there: all of these get in the way. There is no easy, unambiguous way to cultivate tolerance for ambiguity. Perhaps at most we can make a start by recognizing the need and recognizing the dangers to a free society when the demand for quick and easy solutions prevails.

DEEP APPRECIATION FOR THE REQUIREMENTS OF FREEDOM

Janis Joplin had it wrong with her notion that freedom is just another word for nothing left to lose. Quite the contrary: freedom is the basic word for just about everything there is to lose. Without freedom, we might be alive, but we won't have much of a life. To exercise freedom—"the condition of being able to choose and to carry out purposes"—three conditions must be in play: "absence of external constraints," "actual ability with available means," and "power of conscious choice between significant, known alternatives."[13]

Tocqueville saw freedom in America as absence of constraint. "A particular person conceives the thought of some undertaking; . . . the idea of addressing himself to the public authority does not occur to him. He makes known his plan, offers to execute it, calls individual forces to the assistance of his, and struggles hand to hand against all obstacles." The overall benefit is clear, Tocqueville says: "In the long term the general result of all the individual undertakings far exceeds what the government could do."[14]

We know of course that freedom cannot be exercised without some constraints. There must be some tension between freedom and order. For example, when driving a car, we do not run red lights, and we support penalties for those who do; we are willing to trade the freedom to drive however we want in order to have some order, the security of knowing we are much less likely to be in an accident while going through an intersection.

We want to live in a free a society; freedom is obviously necessary for a free society, and freedom is what we think we have. We see and accept what we think are acceptable constraints in terms of the freedom–order tension, and we see little else in the way of what might be unacceptable constraints.

We like our freedom. But it is unfortunately all too easy to go from liking freedom to taking freedom for granted (have we not, we think, always been the freest nation in the world?) to complacency and negligence, a lack of awareness of what we have. It is easy to get used to things. For example, if you enter a house where bread is being baked, the aroma at first is noticeable, but after a minute or two, the aroma is not sensed because of olfactory dullness. To pick up the aroma again, we first have to go outside and then come back into the house. The dulling of smell might be an advantage, as we know when we enter a place with foul odors, odors that usually don't register after a minute or two.

To miss the smell of bread is of little import. To become unaware of freedom and the conditions for freedom is or should be of major concern. Freedom is always in danger, and complacency always increases the danger, the likelihood that freedom will be extinguished. The danger to freedom is that suggested by twentieth-century French philosopher, Raymond Aron. He argued that "it is not enough to have the institutions of freedom: elections, parties, a parliament. Men must have a certain taste for independence, a certain sense of resistance to power, for freedom to be authentic."[15] To speak of the need for resistance to power is to argue that there is indeed power that needs to be resisted. What might that power consist of, and how does it threaten freedom?

External power in the form of an invading army obviously threatens the freedom of people in the country being overrun, and the "certain sense of resistance to power" is manifested in mobilizing armed forces and fighting the invaders. But we also have to recognize the workings of internal power, that is, power exercised by the government in any political entity. Where the internal threats to freedom come from depends on the character of the government. If the government is a kind of dictatorship, then the power is hard force, government surveillance of the people, secret police, informers. Resistance to this kind of power has to take the form of underground movements, possibly a coup.

But if the government is a kind of democracy, a democratic republic of sorts, then freedom can be threatened by nonforceful means. The forms these threats can take have been memorably described by Tocqueville. He speaks of a new kind of despotism, one "more extensive and milder," one that would "degrade men without tormenting them." This soft kind of despotism emerges from the tendency of any government to expand control over people. The soft despotism, the "paternal power" Tocqueville speaks of, ostensibly has in view the happiness of the people. It is fine for the people to enjoy themselves, "provided they think only of enjoying themselves." The soft despotism "facilitates their pleasures, conducts their principal affairs, directs their industry, regulates their estates, divides their inheritances; can it not take away from them entirely the trouble of thinking and the pain of living?"[16]

In our own time, we are confronted with all sorts of government attempts to control behavior. For example, cigarette smoking is not made illegal, but a high "sin tax" is created with the intent of forcing a smoker to quit or at least cut down. We accept the strategy: after all, there is a high cost to society when many people smoke and contract cancer or heart disease as a result. But it is not much of a step from wanting to control cigarette smoking to want to control other behaviors the government deems negative.

Various municipalities have enacted laws to require sunscreen at summer camps, limit toys that can be handed out at fast food restaurants, control the size of soft drink servings, require cars to not have excess mud, and more.[17] In Japan, the government attempts to control obesity by fining companies that fail to reduce the number of obese workers on their payroll.[18]

A problematic characteristic of governmental intrusion to control or modify behavior is the tendency for policies to lead to other policies, each the apparent logical step of the one preceding it. For example, a law requiring companies to treat employees in a given way or face legal penalties will quite reasonably lead to establishment of an enforcement bureaucracy, mandatory reviews of treatment, reports to be filed and reviewed. Moreover, concerns about equality of treatment across companies will quite reasonably lead to further attempts at standardization, and further delineation of rules and regulations.

Perhaps the most obvious recent example of the tension between government, public health, and what is seen as individual freedom is the debate over ways to deal with the Covid-19 pandemic. To wear a mask is seen by many as a desirable behavior that should indeed be regulated and enforced by the government; for others, mask-wearing regulations are one more example of nanny state governmental intrusion. Closure of restaurants and other facilities open to the public is seen either as reasonable and prudent in the face of another wave of the virus or as an overreach, with the government intruding in the private affairs of private enterprise and limiting the freedom of both owners of the facilities and those who might choose to use them.

The concerns of the government for national security are another area of tension. After various terrorist attacks, most notably the 9–11 attacks, debates over the proper balance between freedom and order were resolved in favor of order. What one could carry onto a plane was no longer a matter of personal choice but what the TSA decided to allow.

The encroachments on freedom can come with the best of intentions and sometimes with less than the best. Attention must be paid to Aron's admonition that we maintain a "certain sense of resistance to power." At the same time, surely not all governmental intrusion is an unwelcome attack on freedom. Governmental regulations of coal mining, or pharmacies, or food production seem to make sense for most of us. We welcome safety standards for children's nightwear; we welcome requirements for safety glass. The 1954 Brown decision on desegregating schools is seen by most of us as a welcome governmental intrusion in the name of justice and not as a nanny state dictate.[19]

If anything, then, we are back to the notion of tolerance for ambiguity. Some governmental curtailment of freedom can be justified. And some governmental curtailment of freedom can and perhaps should be justifiably opposed. Above all, however, the threats to freedom are always with us, and a free society demands a citizenry that is always prepared to talk, to consider, and also to provide, where needed, resistance to power. We will do well to recall the words of Frederick Douglass: "Power concedes nothing without a demand. . . . The limits of tyrants are prescribed by the endurance of those whom they oppress."[20]

NEED FOR LONG-TERM TIME FRAME

We have discussed the need for leaders to have a long-term time frame while not overlooking the need to keep a sharp focus on the immediate. Citizens in a free society have a similar need. The importance of a long-term time frame warrants some repetition of what was discussed earlier.

It is tempting to forgo the long-term and plump for the immediate return. Deferred gratification can indeed be gratifying, but there is also something compelling about the notion of a bird in the hand being worth more than two in the bush. The demands of the immediate, the demands of the immediately needful, often take precedence over some far-off abstract future. We do not have to accept the notion of a universal hierarchy of needs to recognize that most of us most of the time have priorities: we need food, we need shelter, we need security, we need a job in order to deal with those priorities.

Because most of us have limited resources and not that much extra, the jobs we have are not guaranteed to last, and when things go wrong—as they will—there are no extra caches of money to cover the unexpected bills, it makes pretty good sense to focus on what you have to do right now. A mortgage payment coming due and a car that won't start will get attention, and if somehow taxes can be reduced (because it is either pay the taxes or fix the car), so much the better.

It is indeed important to have a long-term time perspective. We all live on this Earth, our only home, and the only way our Earth is going to allow future generations to live in at least reasonably good health is to make the long-term investments necessary to deal with climate change and ensure clean water and air. But if citizens are going to be expected to have or develop that long-term time perspective, it is important to first recognize that there are legitimate reasons for many to opt for policies of wealth distribution that will help deal with short-term needs. For many, there will be tensions between those legitimate reasons and what they also realize are important long-term perspectives.

As we all continue with efforts to shift and expand time perspectives, we might consider that there is something incongruous and unfair about asking people who are barely able to make it from paycheck to paycheck to make quick turns to thinking about three generations ahead, while many executives in many companies continue to turn away from that far-in-the-future perspective in order to meet the insistent demands of shareholders for immediate higher dividends. We all need to shift and expand time perspectives. In the course of trying to talk with each other—people we know, people we don't know—we need always to be aware of just who is being asked to do what, and what the costs to people actually are.

These are real world practical matters that need to be addressed if we are serious about changing time perspective. Opportunities and capabilities to act on those opportunities are available variously depending on financial circumstances. For example, many parents would like to be involved in their child's school as a volunteer or tutor or as part of evening fundraisers and other events. Parents with ample and assured resources have no problem getting to the school and joining in. Parents who are working two jobs with long commutes from one to the other might have the same desire to participate as the wealthier parents, but the opportunities are just not there.

If we wish to see all citizens develop a better time perspective, then the differential access question must be addressed. It can be relatively easy to get some groups of people involved. Folks with money and a fair amount of discretionary time will be glad to show up for, say, a series of workshops and programs on the whys and wherefores of time perspective. But left out will be those who are working those two jobs and still trying to find the time to deal with all of the other matters of household economics, health care, car repair—all of those matters that require money and time. Time is a critical variable. It takes a lot more time to get things done when you're poor than it does when you have a lot of money.

So that wonderful series of events on time perspective conceived and put on with the best of intentions may work: most of those who attend will find some enlightenment and will take seriously the challenges of a longer perspective. Follow-up evaluations will be positive. But that group of attendees will be in the minority. Many of those had no chance of attending and thus had no chance to be persuaded. Their views will likely not change, and many will likely find the pleas for the long term interesting but ultimately irrelevant, with short-term politicians speaking in terms they understand and support. In any such political and educative effort, those in this latter group will always far outnumber those who have the resources and time to attend, a fact that politicians and other leaders know and respect.

It should be noted that we do not get around the problem of differential attendance by holding small-group workshops and seminars for those who have comfortable financial resources and doing mass mailings to those whose finances prevent them from attending. This kind of split in attention and effort will simply exacerbate the problem. Those unable to attend will likely not be all that persuaded by a group email and a link to a website featuring time perspectives. Moreover, many might find that, not for the first time, there is a two-tiered effort—one for the wealthy, a lesser one for the less wealthy—a finding hardly likely to encourage widespread involvement.

If serious efforts at changing time perspective are to have any chance of succeeding, careful attention must be paid to finding ways to bring together all people in a given target area so that they can all talk with each other.

BEHAVING IN AND TOWARD A MORE THOUGHTFUL PUBLIC

As discussed briefly in chapters 1 and 3, a more thoughtful public is a critical element of a free society. Just how critical can be seen by comparing a more thoughtful public to its superficially similar but far different relative, a persuaded audience. A persuaded audience is the target of one-way communication from a leader or leaders. The audience is passive, accepting what it is told. The acceptance can be enthusiastic—at least on the surface—as can be seen in newsreel footage of Stalin's speeches or the Nuremberg rallies in Nazi Germany in the 1930s. Or the audience can be cowed, or fearful, or secretly resentful.

No matter the actual audience response, the communication is one way. Those in the audience listen to speech from a leader. They usually do not talk with each other while in the role of audience. At most, they may in various nonformal or sometimes furtive ways talk with others about what was said by the leader.

A more thoughtful public, on the other hand, has multiple interactions between leaders and citizens and between citizens and other citizens at its core. Citizens listen to and speak with leaders, leaders respond, and citizens are free to talk with each other, individually or in groups. The listening and speaking is multidirectional and dynamic, leading to or as part of the process of thinking and judging past and future policies and directions. A more thoughtful public involves acting in concert and as such draws on skills of listening and speaking, skills that are part of the ongoing development of social capital.

Of the many features of a more thoughtful public, we can consider two in further detail: the act of active listening and the need for reference to both the past and the future when considering past and future policies.

THE ACT OF ACTIVE LISTENING

We need to listen to others. Our listening takes various forms and has various purposes. Sometimes we listen to get information we think we need. Sometimes we listen to others because they are talking and we want to at least appear to be interested: to appear not to listen is the act of a boor or a political opponent. Sometimes we listen to others because they are asking for our help or our support or our sympathy. Sometimes our formal role in an organization includes at least pro forma listening: a city council member or a member of a school board is expected to listen to perhaps many hours of testimony.

No matter what our situation or our purposes, when we listen, we sometimes tend to make two kinds of errors. One kind of error involves mistaken understanding. We listen to someone tell us about a problem they are having. Before the person has gone very far into the details, we stop listening because we think we understand what the problem is and we have already determined a problem-solving response.

We stop because we recognize the pattern and we know the answer the pattern usually dictates. Ironically, the greater our experience with problem situations, the greater our skills at pattern recognition, and thus the increased likelihood of stopping listening. When we stop listening, we often miss picking up minor but critical details. The pattern we so quickly spotted is the correct one, except for those minor details, and it might turn out that our solution is quite off the mark.

The second kind of error involves listening with the intent of spotting an opening so you can say what is on your mind. Perhaps you are anxious to get on with it: you want to say something, you are enthusiastic. Or perhaps you simply know you are correct and the other person is blathering on and on and needs to be stopped. For whatever reason, there is no serious listening here, no attempt at seriously trying to hear and understand a point of view. All that matters is deciding when you can politely jump in and make your point.

Active listening, on the other hand, asks much more of us. Active listening asks us to actually pay attention. We have to hear other people out, not for the purpose of agreeing or disagreeing with them, but in order to understand what they are saying. Imagine a clutch of people who have volunteered to serve on a school district advisory committee to consider student safety issues. At the initial meeting, the school district superintendent asks each member to say why they agreed to serve. The first person to speak up says that she is there because the district needs armed guards in the schools.

The very next person speaks up, saying that he is there because the most dangerous thing they could do would be to put armed guards in the schools. There might seem to be an impasse here: she has her opinion, he has his, and the listening stops. At this point, though, the superintendent, listening with care to both speakers, might note that however the two might disagree, they actually agree on a deeper and more significant matter: both have the safety of students as a very high and nonnegotiable priority.

Active listening and the search for common ground take time. The initiator of the group, the superintendent, could decide to save time by curtailing the introductory activities. As quite often happens, the superintendent could simply say, "Let's go around the table and introduce ourselves," and each person will give their name and nothing more. Perhaps some time has been saved in the short run, but what has been denied is the opportunity for the group members to get to know each other and learn what they are concerned about. The shortcut approach is usually not productive: what with the inevitable differences in perspective, the group will not be likely to develop a common understanding and consensus about safety policies.

Active listening, whether at a school district committee meeting, a city council meeting, or a neighborhood block watch meeting on crime concerns, involves seeking common ground and taking the necessary time to seek it. Common ground is not always to be found; it is not an elixir. But the search for common ground as part of people getting to know—and quite possibly to trust—each other is critical and worth the time.

THE NEED FOR A CAREFUL VIEW TOWARD THE PAST AND TOWARD THE FUTURE

Unless plagued with deficient memory, we have some sense of history, some sense of who we are and where we are and how we got this way. We can look back on how we have lived, what decisions we have made; we focus on our individual pleasures and regrets, while thinking about what we might do differently in the days ahead. This kind of personal looking back is exemplified by the elderly physician in Ingmar Bergman's film *Wild Strawberries*, the butler in Kazuo Ishiguro's book *The Remains of the Day*, and Frank Sinatra's songs "My Way" and "It Was a Very Good Year."

These personal reflective journeys to the past are important, and even if we do not subscribe fully to the notion that the unexamined life is not worth living, we might well agree that the unexamined life is a life not well lived.

But there is another kind of looking back, a collective looking back as a group to shared memories and beliefs. That collective memory is important for group cohesion. Certainly in the context of a free society, it is important that we have a good sense of the past—what we were and how we[#]came to be who we are—as we listen and speak together to understand the present and look to how we might plan the future. Perhaps even more important, a careful look back might serve as a kind of radar warning, an alert that we are drifting, through inattention or bad decision making or both, away from what we were and might want to be.

These benefits of looking carefully at the past are discussed in as discerning a way as can be found by Ralph Lerner in his *Revolutions Revisited*, with discussions of how three statesmen—Edmund Burke, Abraham Lincoln, and Alexis de Tocqueville—with conscious deliberation, helped their people advert to the past. Although they differ in specific approaches, the three "portray a past worth living up to and give heart to the living generation to claim that legacy as their own by right."[21]

Although all three have in mind the need for corrective action by a people slipping away from what they could and should be, that need is not made known through harsh criticism and moralizing from on high. "You people are bad, you should be ashamed of yourselves, and you need to do better" rarely moves people to authentic self-contemplation.

Rather, Burke and Lincoln and Tocqueville find ways to remind the people of who they once were, a prideful legacy, as the beginnings of considering the present. As Lincoln puts it, "we are not what we have been." Lerner tells us that Lincoln is "calling for America to return to its promise." The approach is "an invocation of a past, addressed to the present, on behalf of a future generation."[22]

In many respects, this approach to the past is invoked by Langston Hughes in one of his greatest poems: "Let America be America again; Let it be the dream it used to be."[23] And, from a slightly different perspective, from present to future, we are reminded of Winston Churchill's invocation in one of his finest war speeches: "Let us brace ourselves to our duty, and so bear ourselves that if the British Empire and its Commonwealth last a thousand years, men will still say, 'this was their finest hour.'"[24]

The invocation of the past as a corrective for the present, Lerner carefully reminds us, is not easy to do well. It is necessary to "inspirit without appearing to be merely hectoring, to embolden without abetting recklessness and impatience, to foster deliberation without forgetting the need for decisive action."[25]

The task of invoking the past in useful ways is made even more difficult given the ideas of the past many people already carry with them. Many people are willing to be reminded of the greatness of the past—as long as it is *their* fondly cherished past. And for some, as per William Faulkner's observation, "the past is never dead. It's not even past."[26] As such, many people might well agree with Langston Hughes: they, too, want America to be America again, but what they want to recover is an America of lynchings, strict segregation, and people knowing and keeping their place.

Without some clear specification of what it is we are supposed to return to, the invocation of return makes everybody feel good as they apply their own Rorschach test to the matter. Consider the main rhetorical invocation of Donald Trump's 2016 presidential campaign, "Make America Great Again." It was an invocation, a reminder that we are not now as we once were, but we can (or I can make you) become great again.

There is another confounding difficulty in useful invocation of the past. Lerner concludes his analysis by asking whether invoking past greatness will "inspire further acts of greatness, or only make comparable efforts seem less needful." There is no pat answer: "Through their deeds their living and the unborn would answer that for themselves."[27]

Beyond these choices to be made, we can see a further difficulty. Celebrating the greatness of the past might for some simply be depressing or a reminder of inadequacies. A baseball stadium flies with pride banners proclaiming a team's going to the playoffs in years past, but when there are only four banners displayed, and the latest such banner is dated 2001, all this display of pride does for many fans is remind them of subsequent disaster years with no end in sight, just two decades of promises of "building years." Instead of inspiring to do better, the invocation of past greatness can provoke many to simply give up on a task that seems way past any chance of being accomplished.

There are dangers, then, with the strategy of invoking the past as a corrective to present actions and as a guide to future policies. These dangers do not mean that the strategy should be discarded, only that the strategy must be used with care. For the strategy to make sense, people will have to be able to think clearly. As they listen—actively listen—to leaders and fellow citizens advert to past greatness, they will have to exercise a certain moderate skepticism.

Their skepticism must be somewhere in the middle between the extreme of believing nothing one hears and the extreme of believing everything one hears. If we have a surfeit of skepticism, we will believe nothing other than that everybody who tells us anything is out to take advantage of us or is otherwise worthless. To believe everything with no critical lens, on the other hand, is to be fair game for con artists and liars of all kinds, with birthrights sold not even for a mess of pottage.

To look to the past, to understand the present, and to plan with caution and care the future, the first order of business is to think clearly, think for ourselves, and develop habits of mind that will prevent self-illusion.

WHAT PEOPLE MUST EXPECT OF LEADERS IN AND FOR A FREE SOCIETY

It is fitting that the following brief discussion of expectations of leaders should reflect what the people must expect of themselves. What has been emphasized throughout this volume is the relational function of leadership, the notion that a more thoughtful public in a free society is going to expect and deserve critical interaction between leaders and people, an interaction that also involves a great deal of interaction among the people themselves. That said, some expectations can be put on the table. The list is not long, but the expectations are demanding. Citizens must expect that they will not be lied to. This may seem like a reasonable expectation, one that might go without saying, but while leadership lying is not new, surely such behavior has moved to new lows in recent years.[28] To lie to people or to hide bad news from people is to say that people are gullible or weak ninnies who can't handle the truth. In this world we more or less get what we ask for. If a leader treats people like sheep, sooner or later some people might lower themselves to meet expectations, while others will respond with quiet resentment or will simply ignore the leader. None of these behaviors do much for supporting a free society.

Leaders in a free society will, within the bounds of national security, take people into their confidence and share with them the threatening as well as the reassuring. Winston Churchill certainly shared both the bad and the good. Consider, too, President Kennedy's Inaugural Address, on one hand offering hope and a positive message while at the same time sharing a negative message: "We are called to bear the burden of a long twilight struggle, year in and year out, 'rejoicing in hope, patient in tribulation'—a struggle against the common enemies of man: tyranny, poverty, disease, and war itself."

President Kennedy realized that he could not ask people to be strong in the face of a "long twilight struggle" if his speech implied they were fragile ninnies. If he had lied to people by saying everything would be just fine, that the people would win so much they would tire of winning, he could not at the same time expect them to be strong.

Citizens have a right to expect clear and comprehensive knowledge of what their leaders are doing both in public and offstage. This is not a right to be given them (and thus possibly be taken away) by leaders. In the urgent phrasing of John Adams, citizens "have a right, an indisputable, unalienable, indefeasible divine right to that most dreaded, and envied kind of knowledge, I mean of the characters and conduct of their rulers."[29] If people are to make wise decisions about leaders and policies and future directions of a free society, if they are to think for themselves, they must have all available information.

Citizens must expect that leaders will not appeal to the worst in people, or even the average in us, but must appeal to the best and appeal to how we might rise above that best. Again, President Kennedy in his Inaugural Address advises: "Ask of us [leaders] the same high standards of strength and sacrifice which we ask of you."

NOTES

1. Ralph Lerner, *Revolutions Revisited: Two Faces of the Politics of Enlightenment* (Chapel Hill: University of North Carolina Press, 1994), 31.

2. Alexis de Tocqueville, "To Claude-François de Corcelle, September 17, 1853," in *Selected Letters on Politics and Society*, ed. Roger Boesche, trans. James Toupin and Roger Boesche (Berkeley: University of California Press, 1985), 294.

3. Fyodor Dostoevsky, *The Brothers Karamazov*, trans. Richard Pevear and Larissa Volokhonsky (San Francisco: North Point Press, 1990), 44.

4. Francis Bacon, "Of Simulation and Dissimulation," in *The Essays*, ed. John Pitcher (London: Penguin Books, 1985), 76.

5. Edward Gibbon, *The History of the Decline and Fall of the Roman Empire*, ed. David Womersley (London: Penguin Press, 1995), 2:213.

6. Francis Fukuyama, *Identity: The Demand for Dignity and the Politics of Resentment* (New York: Farrar, Straus and Giroux, 2018), 122–23. On identity and identity politics, see also Mark Lilla, *The Once and Future Liberal: After Identity Politics* (New York: Harper, 2018).

7. Fukuyama, *Identity*, 128–31.

8. Fukuyama, *Identity*, 131.

9. Fukuyama, *Identity*, 131.

10. On the behavior of British people during World War II, see Philip Ziegler, *London at War 1939–1945* (New York: Knopf, 1995).

11. An earlier but still useful discussion of open systems can be found in Daniel Katz and Robert L. Kahn, *The Social Psychology of Organizations* (New York: Wiley, 1966).

12. For a comprehensive review of the research literature on the construct of tolerance of ambiguity, see Adrian Furnham and Joseph Marks, "Tolerance of Ambiguity: A Review of Recent Literature," *Psychology* 04 (September 2013): 717–28.

13. Herbert J. Muller, *Issues of Freedom: Paradoxes and Promises* (New York: Harper & Brothers, 1960), 5.

14. Alexis de Tocqueville, *Democracy in America*, trans. Harvey C. Mansfield and Delba Winthrop (Chicago: University of Chicago Press, 2000), 90.

15. Raymond Aron, *Main Currents in Sociological Thought*, trans. Richard Howard and Helen Weaver (New York: Doubleday, 1968), 274.

16. Tocqueville, *Democracy in America*, 663. For a discerning discussion of Tocqueville's approach to soft despotism, see Paul A. Rahe, *Soft Despotism, Democracy's Drift: Montesquieu, Rousseau, Tocqueville, and the Modern Prospect* (New Haven: Yale University Press, 2009).

17. See William Haupt III, "Op Ed: The 2020 Nanny State—The Good, the Bad and the Ugly," *The Center Square*, January 6, 2020, https://www.thecentersquare.com/national/op-ed-the-2020-nanny-state-the-good-the-bad-and-the-ugly/article_1031d970-308f-11ea-b471-174f6aadaa8a.html.

18. See Louise Stephen, "Obesity in Japan: Can the Metabo Law Prevent It?" February 24, 2018, https://louisestephen.com/2018/02/24/obesity-japan-can-metabo-law-prevent-it/.

19. For a discussion of benefits of governmental intrusion, see Simon Chapman, "One Hundred and Fifty Ways the Nanny State is Good for Us," *The Conversation*, July 1, 2013, https://theconversation.com/one-hundred-and-fifty-ways-the-nanny-state-is-good-for-us-15587.

20. Frederick Douglass, "West India Emancipation" (speech, Canandaigua, New York, August 3, 1857), University of Rochester Frederick Douglass Project, https://rbscb.lib.rochester/4398.

21. Lerner, *Revolutions Revisited*, 131.

22. Lerner, *Revolutions Revisited*, 93, 132.

23. For Langston Hughes's poem "Let America Be America Again," see *The Collected Poems of Langston Hughes* (New York: Knopf, 1994), https://poets.org/poem/let-america-be-america-again.

24. Winston Churchill's "Their Finest Hour" speech on June 18, 1940, can be found in many places. See, for example, International Churchill Society, https://winstonchurchill.org/resources/speeches/1940-the-finest-hour/their-finest-hour/.

25. Lerner, *Revolutions Revisited*, 132.

26. William Faulkner, *Requiem for a Nun* (New York: New American Library, 1954), 229.

27. Lerner, *Revolutions Revisited*, 134.

28. For a useful overview, see Eric Alterman, *When Presidents Lie: A History of Official Deception and Its Consequences* (New York: Viking, 2004).

29. John Adams, "Dissertation on the Canon and the Feudal Law," in Papers of John Adams, eds. Robert J. Taylor et al., vol. 1, no. 3 (Cambridge: Belknap Press, 1977), 121.

Chapter 5

Schools and the Sustaining of a Free Society

We have been bequeathed a free society, and to varying degrees all of us enjoy its benefits. We did precious little to deserve what was bequeathed. What we did deserve, we deserved simply because we were human beings. The free society was, again in varying degrees, simply there. We come into the world with much going on of which we know little. As we grow older, we learn more about our rights in a free society. And we learn, again in varying degrees, our responsibilities to act in that free society, to improve it, to secure its benefits for all people.

One of those responsibilities is to sustain what we have and to ensure that those coming after us will have the same opportunities to enjoy and improve that bequeathed to them. We cannot guarantee that future generations will value and improve and sustain the free society that is now theirs. We can only do the best we can, hoping that they come to understand what they have, just as the generations before us hoped the same of us.

The responsibilities of a free society and the conditions necessary to secure and sustain it must be learned. We may have inherent rights, but we do not at birth have the knowledge; the skills in "listening and speaking, thinking and judging" and the moral grounding that must accompany acquisition of that knowledge and skills. It is clear that learning must take place. What is less clear are the corollary questions. Who is to learn what? And where is this desired learning to take place?

There are some areas of human endeavor where the answers to "who is to learn what and where?" are reasonably straightforward. Consider, for example, the learning necessary for the practice of medicine. Because the learning required is so extensive and complex, and so costly to provide and attain, we take it for granted that only those who have the very high intelligence and the very high commitment to medical practice should be given the opportunity to learn. As for where the learning is take place, there is general agreement about specialized places—medical schools, teaching hospitals, clinics. As for the "what" of the learning, there is general agreement among specialists: a common general medical learning plus a good deal of learning in one or more of the specialties.

There is general agreement among all of us regarding the limits and constraints of medical education. We do not expect everyone in our country to become a physician. We do expect that medical school admissions decisions be based on relevant matters of merit—intelligence, commitment, probability of completion. And we certainly expect irrelevant factors such as ethnicity and gender to have no part in the decision process. We understand the need for caps on enrollment. We do not need to produce hundreds of thousands of physicians every year, nor can we afford to do so.

But when we turn from the relatively straightforward need for selectivity and specialized learning of medicine (or, if we wish, any other profession or occupation requiring specialized knowledge) to the learning required for securing and sustaining a free society, the "who is to learn what and where?" matter becomes much more complex. Not everyone is to be a physician. But everyone is and will continue to be a participant in society. And, assuming we wish to secure and sustain a free society wherein all are active and responsible citizens, then we need to consider what learning is commonly needed for all. Further, assuming that it is important that *all* of the young acquire the learning we deem necessary, where is it most likely that all will indeed do so?

Even assuming we all are committed in one way or another to a free society and that all the young learn what we deem necessary, we must again consider that there is likely not full agreement as to all of the elements of a free society and as to what roles we all are to play in that society. There are those who believe that even in a relatively free society, there are those who are leaders and there are those who, unable or unwilling to be leaders, are content with following along. For those holding these kinds of beliefs, the matter of citizenship education and who is to learn what and where is not all that vexing.

Most of the top few (by birth or by some sort of merit) are to receive one kind of citizenship education. They go to the selective schools, continue to learn and be socialized into their leadership roles, and then get on with the business of running things. As for all the others, citizenship education is likewise straightforward. All that is needed, one supposes, is knowing the Pledge of Allegiance and the Star Spangled Banner.

Belief that a free society is good but is best when the few are free to run things while the many are free to go along is a belief held by some now, a belief held by some in past years. Tocqueville was alert to this belief in Jacksonian America. He observed that many of the wealthy publicly extolled the "advantages of democratic forms," but "it is easy to perceive in the rich a great disgust for the democratic institutions of their country. The people are a power that they fear and scorn."[1]

But if we argue, and believe, that in a good free society, all are citizens capable of and willing to assume the rights and responsibilities of citizenship, then we have to consider the matter of who is to learn what and where in terms of *all*. We are talking, then, about learning common to all, knowledge common to all, attitudes common to all. What should all learn? And where are all to learn what is necessary?

Some of what the young need to learn can be dealt with at home or through involvement with religious institutions. But if we want to ensure that the greatest possible proportion of the young learn what is necessary, then we must turn our attention to the public schools. No other societal agency can approximate what the public schools can do to provide the necessary knowledge—and the appropriate socialization and valuing—necessary.

There are no guarantees, of course. Human variation being what it is, not everyone will emerge from the public schools with all that we might hope. Some of the young will drop out of school. Others may stay but ignore or remain impervious to the teachings about a free society. Still others may acquire some of the appropriate knowledge but will be unwilling or unable to become socialized or to value a free society. That said, the public schools still stand as the societal agency most capable of providing what we—and the young—need.

If we are to rely on schools to provide the opportunities for all of the young to develop the working knowledge we deem essential, then we must have a clear understanding of the nature of schools and the systems of which schools are a part. We are asking a good deal of the schools. We must know what we are asking. We must assess the reasonableness of our requests. We must be able to understand the responses of the schools. We must be able to review and judge the effectiveness of those we have entrusted to run the schools. We must be able to do all of these, and we must be able to do all of these with thoughtfulness. We will not be able to do these things in any thoughtful way without having a clear understanding of how schools function.

It is a challenge for many to develop that clear understanding. Our own experiences of schooling and our memories of what we think those experiences were at once convince us that we know what we need to know about schools. And once we think we have sufficient knowledge of schools—or any topic—we tend to stop asking questions and stop learning. Our memories can be faulty here. A 1902 editorial in the New York *Sun* announced with certainty that "when we were boys, boys had to do a little work in school. They were not coaxed; they were hammered. . . . And you had to learn."[2] With our sometimes faulty memories, schooling in *our* time back then was rigorous, we were expected to work hard, and so we did, we think, much more so than in the current easy times where standards are low and shoddy performance is overlooked.

As such, part of our effort to develop a good understanding of schools must begin with being skeptical about the understanding we think we have and being skeptical about our memories. Being duly skeptical, we can move on to developing a basic familiarity with elementary facts and figures about the schools, their scope, how they are funded, how they are run. In what follows, we consider very briefly some of the scope and some of the constraints of the American schooling system.

There are some 3.2 million K-12 teachers in public schools; there are 500,000 teachers in private schools. Although widely varying from state to state and widely varying depending on years of experience, teachers on the average earn some $42,000 per year. There are approximately 50.7 million students in K-12 public schools. There is an additional 5.7 million in private schools. Overall annual expenditures for public schools are approximately $720 billion. Of that $720 billion, the federal government provides about 9 percent. There are some 13,800 local public school districts, governmental entities created by and under the supervision of the several states. States and local school districts provide most of the funding for schools; monies are generated by property taxes, excise and other taxes, and local school tax levies.[3]

There are a good many implications that can be derived from these skeletal data. Consider the number of K-12 teachers: 3.7 million. This is a considerable multiple when trying to work through all sorts of budget and policy issues. For example, it is sometimes heard that we would have better teachers in America if we were to pay teachers higher salaries. Some of the best and the brightest that are currently going into other fields would be willing to go into teaching if the pay were better. Let us set aside for the moment the assumptions being made by this argument's proponents and look just at the financial implications. We would have to have a considerable increase in pay in order to attract those currently going elsewhere. A thousand-dollar increase would not do the trick. Perhaps a ten-thousand-dollar increase might make a difference. With 3.7 million as our multiple, a ten-thousand-dollar increase means finding an additional $37 billion annually. Knowing what the multiple is surely will help us leave vague generalities aside ("let's just pay teachers more") in favor of hard facts.

It should be noted that those who choose to go into teaching do so because they want to teach. Most everybody thinking of entering the world of education is aware of the pay scales. Some matters that many intending teachers are not aware of are the constraints put on public school teachers. Those going into teaching will do well to be aware of these constraints in advance in order to avoid unpleasant surprises and perhaps unpleasant decisions that might have to be made. But all of us—those of us constituting a more thoughtful public—also need to be aware of these constraints as part of our basic understanding of how schools work so we can keep our expectations on firm ground.

Public school teachers are necessarily in six kinds of relationships. First, teachers are in a relationship with the state government. As state agents employed by the state, teachers have to deal with curriculum and pedagogy mandates of the state. They have to comply with state testing requirements. They have to comply with all the other rules and regulations promulgated by the state. Such rules and regulations are extensive. For example, in Washington State, the portions of published versions of the Revised Code and the Administrative Code pertaining to schooling run to more than twelve hundred pages. Second, teachers are in a relationship with the federal government, again having to maintain compliance with a host of rules and regulations. Third, teachers are in a relationship with the local school district in which they are employed.

Fourth, teachers are in a relationship with students, parents, and other community members; teachers must constantly be dealing with a wide variety of expectations and demands. Fifth, teachers are in a relationship with others in the workplace, a professional relationship, to be sure, but also a competitive relationship because of always-scarce resources. Sixth, teachers are in a relationship to their profession, that is, they act in relation to their collective image of the norms of teaching.[4]

Given these complicated and interwoven relationships, we can see that the notion of the independent teacher isolated in his or her classroom doing as he or she sees fit is simply wrong. All public school teachers are constantly negotiating their way through a sometimes bewildering maze of demands and constraints. When we, as a more thoughtful public, try to understand and think through what schools do, and what they might do, we need to keep an awareness of these demands and constraints before us.

Consider other proposals about schools that are sometimes heard. There are those who propose extending the school year. Currently, and for some many decades now, American public school students attend school 180 days per year. In Japan, it will be pointed out, students attend 220 days per year. Surely, some will say, Japan's schools are "better" because of those extra forty days of being in the classroom. Again, let us set aside some of the presumptions and look at the financial implications. For purposes of rapid math, let's say we want our schools to be open to students 216 days rather than 180—a 20 percent increase. Surely we do not expect students just to show up those extra days, sit in classrooms only to play games on their phones. Teachers will have to be there, teaching as per usual, and getting paid as per usual. With our multiple of 3.7 million, those 216 extra days are going to cost a lot.

Another proposal, sometimes just an off-the-cuff solution to school budget problems, is the "cut the fat" from school districts. Surely actual wastage is to be avoided. But we must remind ourselves that on the average, some 80 percent of any school budget goes for salaries and benefits. One can trim a few administrative positions here and there, but if people are looking to make significant budget reductions, very quickly will the question arise as to how many teachers are we to fire. In many school districts, parents and others are clamoring for a reduction of the teacher-pupil ratio, which means clamoring for an increase in the teaching force, not a reduction. We are reminded, then, that education is a labor-intensive occupation.

The skeletal data provided here point out the relatively minor contribution the federal government makes to school district budgets. That 9 percent coming from Washington is not to be tossed aside, of course. But school districts are well aware of the conditions that accompany the offer of federal funds. There are many rules and regulations to be examined and followed, with penalties exacted for noncompliance. In exchange for that relatively minor contribution, many in local school districts find their schools significantly less under their control.

Part of that local control is a result of the larger number of school districts throughout America. The number has actually been reduced over the years. For example, Washington State has some 298 school districts. There were at peak in the 1930s some 1,200 districts. That number was reduced to 498 by the late 1950s.[5] Most of the reduction came through consolidation—elimination of the many one-room schools and the building of high schools requiring greater enrollment levels.

American K-12 public schooling, it can be seen, is a vast enterprise. Due to its size, it does not change quickly. The slowness to change is also due to the school-community culture that has developed since the late 1800s. That culture can be expressed in identifying with the local high school basketball team. And that culture can be expressed in the pride taken in making decisions at the local level about all matters of schooling, from teacher hires, to what the sex education curriculum should include, to football uniforms, and much more—all without interference from the federal government and as little state interference as can be managed.

It is important to understand the schooling system as a vast enterprise overall, but with jealously guarded local control. (After all, despite the obvious respect the Founders had for education, they did not see fit to include any provisions for schooling in the Constitution.) If we are to rely on schools to provide all students with good civic education, we need to understand that our expectations of schools might be met, but only if we have patience and only if we avoid the temptations of top-down directives. Moreover, with this understanding of the basics of schooling, we will be in a much better position to be a more thoughtful public with high—but realistic—expectations of those educators we have entrusted with the work.

Beyond these basics of school operation, we need to consider two other ways to understand the basic functions of schools. As we have noted, no school exists in a vacuum. Schools are part of the systems of school districts and districts are state agencies or corporations; these systems are nested in the larger society. It is reasonable to assume that the objectives and the ways of functioning of schooling systems in any society are in accord with the objectives and ways of functioning in the larger society of which they are a part. After all, schools perform a socialization function, acting to help with development of the young so the young will function effectively as adults. It would be surprising to find a society that had certain aims and values but at the same time supported a schooling system utterly opposed to those aims and values. Congruence is what we would expect to find.

We can look to ancient Sparta as a useful example of high congruence between society and schooling system. A warrior society, Sparta most valued courage, obedience, unquestioned discipline, fighting, and winning—and if not winning, then at least dying gloriously for the cause. A mother might say to her son on leaving for the battlefield, "Return with your shield, or on it." And when we look to Sparta's schooling system, we are not surprised to find an emphasis on war, fighting, courage, cunning, punishment, discipline, unquestioning obedience. Young warriors with a sense of "theirs not to reason why" is what the Spartan regime wanted, and that is what the schools produced.

Another fundamental feature of any schooling system is its sorting function. In American society (as with any society), there are a few good jobs with good remuneration and good working conditions, and then there are many jobs with minimal remuneration and poor working conditions. (I am not speaking in terms of the relative moral worth of work here: in the broad sense, all work is honorable, with the exception of such activities as pimping, child porn, and the like.)

Part of that sorting function involves different kinds of social mobility. Schools can be seen as having a bearing on *place* in society. For some students, schools provide an opportunity to rise, go beyond or above whatever place you or your family is in. Upward mobility is in view here, with parents sharply intent on making sure that both their children and their children's schools do not falter in the mobility stakes—thus the incessant demand for Advanced Placement courses, specialized honors programs, test-taking preparation, and the like. Social mobility can mean moving from lower class to middle class, or middle to high, or high to even higher, and when schools are seen as critical, then all sorts of expenditures can be entailed.

Residents in communities with high concentrations of personal wealth will tax themselves far beyond the average in order to ensure that their local public schools are well supplied with whatever is seen as necessary to help students move along the social mobility path. The drive for social mobility continues from K-12 to higher education and can reach astonishing extremes, as can be seen by the efforts of some parents to spend hundreds of thousands of dollars on illegal efforts to circumvent the regular admissions processes of highly prestigious universities.[6]

For other students, schools serve as a way to remind them of what their place is and the rightness of keeping in that place. It should be noted that both wealthy and low-income students can fall into this category of place maintenance. A wealthy student from a socially prestigious family attending an exclusive private school with others of equal wealth and social prestige finds school a reminder of the place that is deserved, and as preparation for assumption of a high-prestige role in society. Many low-income students also find school a reminder of who and what they will be once they are out in the world: workers, if they can find work, in low-paying jobs with little opportunity for getting ahead. The schools in either case treat students from the perspective of "what you will become determines what you are now."

For all societies, then, schools do many things, but at base they serve a sorting function for the larger society in which they are nested, and there is high congruence between the values and processes of the larger society and the values and processes of the schools.[7]

We have noted that schooling systems are nested in the larger system of American society. To better understand schooling systems and how to work with schools, those of us who constitute a more thoughtful public need to have some basic sense of the larger context, of how critical elements of American society are related to schools.

AMERICAN SOCIETY AS A CONTEXT OF AMERICAN SCHOOLING

If we turn to our own American society, we would hope to find not only a free society, but one open and free to all of its citizens, with equal justice under law, with equitable opportunities to exercise freedom, to design and carry out purposes. We hope to find a free society with equitable opportunities to actively participate in, as we have said, listening and speaking, thinking and judging.

But what we might hope to find and what we in fact find are far apart. Whether we consider family income, family net worth, provision of health care, equal justice under law, or just plain living with a decent sense of security and dignity, the data for as far back as various sets of data have been obtained show clear and consistent and dismaying patterns.

Before proceeding, it is important to be aware of the difficulties involved in trying to consider these patterns and in trying to talk with each other about what cannot help but be seen as downsides of the American current and historic context. In talking of inequalities and inequities in America, it is always difficult to find some middle ground between a general distanced overview of "everybody knows" and feeling the need to find data sources for every claim. As Goethe observed, "Microscopes and telescopes really confuse a man's clear sense of sight."

Further, in talking in particular about the experiences and circumstances of people of any given demographic (ethnicity, gender, social class, and so forth), we must find some middle ground between two extreme positions. In any realm of social science research, it is impossible to make any generalization that applies to all members of a given demographic. Not all women believe or do X. Not all black males experience Y. Not all Pacific Islanders identify themselves as Z.

When faced with the impossibility of total generalization, some people will argue the opposite, saying that if generalizations are impossible, we should consider all people as individuals and ignore group membership or group distinctions. This argument totally denies the existence of groups, of membership in groups, and one's identification with groups—a convenient, but faulty, way out of having to consider any matters dealing with racism, sexism, and other kinds of discrimination.

We must, rather, find the middle ground, going back to the notion of probabilities, of the likelihood of something being experienced by a good many members of a group. There is not room here to even partially review the documentation on discrimination and inequalities in American society. We can, however, remind ourselves of some basic considerations.

We can begin by considering our historical context, the founding of the country, the founding of the republic, in terms of, in Tocqueville's words, "the present state and the probable future of the three races that inhabit the territory of the United States." That is the title of the chapter concluding volume one of *Democracy in America*, a lengthy chapter making up about one-seventh of the entire work. As for the treatment of one of the three races, Tocqueville gives us the horrifying comparison of the Spanish and American conquerors:

> The Spanish unleash their dogs on the Indians as on ferocious beasts; they pillage the New World like a town taken by assault, without discrimination and without pity. . . . The conduct of the Americans in the United States toward the natives, on the contrary breathes the purest love of forms and legality. . . . They

do not permit themselves to occupy their lands without having duly acquired them by means of a contract; and if by chance an Indian nation can no longer live on its territory, they take it like a brother by the hand and lead it to die outside the country of its fathers.

Tocqueville concludes with as powerful a sentence as one is likely to find: "One cannot destroy men while being more respectful of the laws of humanity."[8]

As for the plight of black people in America, and their relationship to white people, Tocqueville saw little hope of resolution. Slavery "is not an institution that can endure," he says; either slaves will end it or masters will. But there is little to suggest to Tocqueville that anything but "great misfortunes" will abound.[9] And thus a country in which land was taken from one group and labor was taken from another group was founded and developed.[10]

And it is not a long way from Tocqueville's America of the early 1830s to the Civil War, to Reconstruction, to de facto re-enslavement of many black Americans, to *Plessy v. Ferguson* in 1896.[11] Separate but hardly equal facilities were with us for another half-century, until being indirectly struck down by the 1954 *Brown v. Board of Education* decision. Another decade passed, with creeping all deliberate speed, until the 1964 Civil Rights Act was pushed through Congress with pressure from civil rights groups and the legislative finesse of Lyndon Johnson.

With regard to the ongoing situation of black people in America, we can consider just one of many indicators of continued systemic racism: the black–white wealth gap. According to the Brookings Institution, as of 2016, there continue to be "staggering racial disparities. At $171,000, the net worth of a typical white family is nearly ten times greater than that of a Black family ($17,150). . . . Gaps in wealth between Black and white households reveal the effects of accumulated inequality and discrimination, as well as differences in power and opportunity that can be traced back to this nation's inception."[12] Progress has been slow in reducing the gaps. "No progress has been made in reducing income and wealth inequalities between black and white households over the past 70 years."[13]

Income disparity is one of many measures of inequality and discrimination. A useful, if distressing, compendium can be found in the *State of Black America*, an annual report issued by the National Urban League, with data on gaps in terms of health care, security, treatment by police, and other measures.[14]

Much of the differential treatment can be seen by the statistical data. And much is surely indicated by reported experiences of racial discrimination, as seen in short form by the prevalence of the phrase "driving while black" or its partner "driving while brown." One finds nowhere in this country the phrase "driving while white," because it is not white drivers who are profiled, stopped, harassed, beaten, and in many cases, killed.

It is no surprise to find, almost on a daily basis, yet another report of discrimination. As yet one more example, in December 2020, the U.S. Air Force inspector general released a report confirming "racial disparities exist for Black members in law enforcement apprehensions, criminal investigations, military justice, administrative separations, placement into occupational career fields, certain promotion rates, professional military educational development, and leadership opportunities."[15] And it is no surprise, then, to find that recent surveys indicate that 62 percent of Americans say that black people contend with "a lot or a great deal of discrimination."[16]

The focus here on Black Americans, albeit brief, is not to suggest that they alone experience inequality and discrimination. Certainly, historically and currently, other groups have in one way or another been denied access. As even a cursory review of a small portion of the literature will suggest, the American experience has been less than satisfactory for many Latinos, Asians, Pacific Islanders, Jews, Catholics, Muslims, and immigrants (especially from non-Anglo-Saxon countries); surely, too, gender and sexual orientation have occasioned discrimination experienced by many.[17]

America for many is indeed the land of opportunity for economic and social gain, the land of immense possibilities. But America is also for many the land of opportunities to be shunned, pushed aside, subjected to "microaggressions" (which are hardly micro when every day without fail one is targeted), threatened, beaten, and killed.

There are two Americas, both lands of opportunities. We can now begin to look at the American schooling system and how it acts in response to these two lands.

INEQUALITY OF ACCESS IN SCHOOLING SYSTEMS

Given what we know of the congruence between society and school, if the American society accepts and often promotes inequalities and discrimination, what might we predict of its schools? If we were to predict that schools would often be places where inequalities and discrimination abounds—with some students benefiting greatly and others left behind and left out—we would be close to the mark.

Again, it is impossible to provide comprehensive or even partial data sets to support the claims regarding the existence and extent of inequalities and discrimination. We can, however, note the statements of two national education organizations as indicative. In speaking to the needs of "historically disadvantaged" children, the National School Boards Association states that

"We recognize that based on factors including but not limited to disability, race, ethnicity, and socioeconomic status, students are deprived of equitable educational opportunities. Educational equity is the intentional allocation of resources, instruction, and opportunities according to need, requiring that discriminatory practices, prejudices, and beliefs be identified and eradicated."[18]

Similarly, the National PTA speaks of its "commitment to diversity, equity and inclusion," and identifies the need to "prioritize and advocate for innovative, sustainable solutions that work for a diverse range of children and families, especially those underrepresented and/or marginalized in our communities." The National PTA argues that "across the country, students, families and educators experience vastly different education systems that either support—or hinder—the ability for all children to reach their full potential. These differences are often due to disparities in opportunities, access and financial resources—and whether or not parents are respected as equal partners in their child's education."[19]

Such statements are not, one might claim, direct empirical proof of lack of equal and equitable access to education, knowledge, and opportunities. But surely the promulgation of such statements points to matters that should be of concern. After all, we know that if there is a commandment or law not to do something, then it is a reasonable presumption that that something has been done, and probably done more than once, and might even still be being done. "Do Not Litter Under Penalty of Law" means people somewhere have been littering.

There are, of course, thousands of reports on thousands of research studies documenting the role schools (and families and communities) play in the two lands of American opportunities. There are many disagreements among thousands of researchers, but there is no disagreement over the basic notion that there are, as the National PTA puts it, "disparities in opportunities, access and financial resources."

The disagreements among researchers are over the extent of the disparities and the relative weight to be assigned to various hypothesized causes and correlates of the disparities. For example, one group of researchers finds that the achievement gap between rich and poor students has not changed much over the past fifty years. Another researcher disagrees with those findings: his analysis suggests that the gap has grown significantly over those same decades.[20] There are technical reasons for the different conclusions: questions of psychometrics, research methodology, and the like. But there is no question that in the American land of two opportunities, the wealthy and the poor experience school differently and are offered different opportunities.[21]

In speaking of these different opportunities, sociologist George Counts put it bluntly: "Why should we provide at public expense these advanced educational opportunities for X because his father is a banker and practically deny them to Y because his father cleans the streets of the city?"[22]

We do not have to review the vast research literature to determine whether or not we wish to recognize the disparities. The disparities are evident, although of course varying from school to school, district to district. But we do have to recognize the disparities. We need to recognize them for ethical reasons: there is something plain wrong about supporting a school system that gives a "good" education to the rich and denies that education to the poor.

Citizens involved in one way or another with the schools do not need to have at hand all of the research findings on the various disparities in the schooling system. They do not need to sort through the many claims and counterclaims of researchers as to just how much variance in achievement can be accounted for by dozens of interrelated factors. Most citizens are not going to be asked to join this or that national commission to study and report on (yet again) why low-income and minority students do less well in school, why resources are allocated inequitably, and so forth.

But, as discussed in the pages below, we can expect citizens to be involved with their local schools and school districts. And as part of that involvement, citizens need to be aware of the ever-present *potential* that some students or some groups of students are being denied opportunities because of all sorts of factors and that denial is unfair and needs attention. It is the potential for denial that should prompt citizens to seek information, to scan the schooling environment.

For example, we know that the 2020 virus pandemic has caused many schools to provide all instruction online. For some families, online work is already commonplace: they have the computers and the connections, and they know how to make things work to zoom right in. But citizens will want to be sure that *all* families are similarly equipped and ready to go. There is always the potential that some families don't have the equipment or the expertise in using the equipment, and it takes active and concerted effort to seek information to make sure that resources are available to all and usable by all. (It will be noted that whatever the availability, poor and non-white students have been more likely to experience learning disruption because of the pandemic than their wealthier white counterparts.)[23]

We say we want *all* of the young to have the necessary working knowledge to be able to act as good citizens in a free society. If schools were the same for all and were equally good for all in providing opportunities to develop the necessary working knowledge irrespective of student gender, ethnicity, financial status, and social class, then we could move quickly to a discussion of curriculum—what should be taught and when. But we also have to address the possibilities of unequal schooling experiences of students. We cannot just drop in a civic education curriculum and expect that all students in the schools will obtain the necessary working knowledge to be good citizens. Many minority and low-income students do less well in English, math, science, and other parts of the curriculum. Why would we expect civic education to be an exception?

We have two tasks. We do indeed need to look at creating a good civic education program that would involve development of curriculum and other kinds of structure learning experiences. But we also need to acknowledge and address the overall problem of potential unequal access and unequal treatment. Does one task have to be dealt with before the other? Do we need to first somehow "fix" the larger system and then turn to design and implementation of the civic education curriculum? Before we can address this question, we need to discuss who is responsible for the two tasks, and we need to discuss in some detail just what the tasks might entail.

WHO IS RESPONSIBLE AND WHAT CAN RESPONSIBLE PEOPLE DO?

In chapter 3, we discussed some of the responsibilities all leaders have for school improvement and for civic education programs. But all of us—leaders and citizens alike—have responsibilities along the lines of the argument presented so far. That argument, in sum, is this: (A) If you agree that a free society must be bequeathed to future generations, and (B) if you agree that future generations must acquire necessary working knowledge so they can secure and sustain a free society and will be able to in turn bequeath it to those coming after them, and (C) if you agree that schools are the most likely place where the greatest proportion of young people can acquire the necessary working knowledge, and (D) if you acknowledge that schools do not do well by many students, particularly ethnic minority students and low-income students, then it is our responsibility to work with the schools to make them better for *all* students and to make sure *all* students are acquiring the necessary working knowledge.

There are many ways for citizens to work with each other and with educators to address the tasks of overall school improvement and development of civic education programs. The following list of six approaches is meant to be illustrative and not all-inclusive.

One way to effect change in local schools is to get appointed or elected to a local school board. There are some 13,800 local school districts, each with a board of directors responsible for setting district policy and hiring administrators to implement those policies. In smaller school districts, an election campaign is not all that expensive. Even in large metropolitan districts, the costs are not prohibitive. A good resource for prospective school board members is the organization mentioned earlier in this chapter—the National School Boards Association.

Not everyone has the time to serve on a school board. But if your situation is such that it's not possible for you to serve, you have other options. You can get together with other people to talk about finding likely candidates and then support their campaigns, and if they win, continue to support them. School board members (as well as administrative staff) are in vulnerable positions. They need support—as long as they do indeed deserve it—especially when some in the district have short time frames, short tempers, and little knowledge of the issues.

A second way to effect change is to work specifically on civic education program development with others and with district educators. This work will likely involve taking a careful look at existing civic education curriculum and other programs. Most districts do offer some courses in U.S. Government, civics, and the like. These may or may not be suitable, but should be reviewed in light of the framework offered in chapter 1 outlining the conditions necessary for a healthy free society.[24]

A third way to effect change is to serve on school district volunteer committees dealing with overall school curriculum, budget, facilities planning, and the like. If such committees don't exist in your school district, work with the school district superintendent, other administrative staff, and board members to create them. Again, you can also talk with others, encouraging them to serve on various volunteer committees. It is particularly important to encourage students to find ways to serve on such committees.

A fourth way to effect change is to sponsor coffee hours in your immediate neighborhood to discuss school issues and concerns. Attendees could be a combination of neighbors (of varying political persuasion) along with district educators, including the superintendent, a school board member, a principal, and a teachers' union member. A classified union member might also be on hand. The district educators are not there to do formal presentations or to try to persuade you and your neighbors of the rightness of district policy but to actively listen to what people have to say. Neighbors can get to know each other better and get to know district educators better as well.

As we have discussed in chapter 4, active listening is key. A district superintendent involved in such coffee hours put it this way: "The core to this work is listening, to be fully present, to see and reflect for others the gifts and talents they have (the potential they have), and to have a profound respect for the dignity and worth of all people. . . . Being fully present means working on getting rid of the chatter in our head, suspending our judgments, attending fully and openly, and working to understand the legitimacy of what the other person is saying."[25]

A fifth way to effect change is to work with school district staff and board to develop appropriate ways to assess and evaluate student progress in acquiring the necessary working knowledge. It is important to make sure all involved understand that scores on standardized achievement tests have little to do with measuring acquisition of the necessary knowledge. There is an old learning measurement notion that applies here: the less important the learning is, the easier it is to measure. It would be easy to measure the extent to which a student learned, say, all fifty state capitals or when a given law was passed. It is far more difficult to measure some of the learnings we have highlighted, such as—back to Raymond Aron—"a certain sense of resistance to power, for freedom to be authentic."[26]

The difficulties notwithstanding, it is critical that citizens and district educators find mutually agreeable ways to assess and understand what is happening (or not happening) in the civic education program and more largely in the schools. Assessment data are needed for pedagogical purposes. More largely, the process of regular assessment of skills, attitudes, and dispositions will serve to remind citizens and educators alike of the importance of civic education.[27]

A sixth way to effect change is to work with teacher education faculty in local colleges and universities. Such work may seem far removed from the immediacy of the day-to-day K-12 classroom, but our concern here is sustaining a free society over time, and our long view needs to recognize what tomorrow's teachers will be doing decades from now. It makes little sense to wait until teachers are in the classroom and then try to make sure those teachers have the requisite knowledge and training to deal with all of the aspects of civic education we say are important. It makes much more sense to develop and sustain teacher education programs in which civic education is seen as a critical part of what every teacher does in the classroom and in the school.[28]

There are many useful consequences emerging from the kinds of citizen involvement outlined here. The first consequence pertains to our question of ordering of tasks—should overall school improvement precede or follow civic education program development? The response, we can argue, is neither. What can happen is that the collective work on the civic education program might serve as an organizing nudge, a way of getting at the larger questions of who has access to what, to questions of disparity and discrimination.

As a part of civic education program development, it is surely reasonable for citizens to express the desire for and the concern over making sure that *all* students, irrespective of family income, gender, ethnicity, or any other possibly extraneous variable, will acquire the necessary working knowledge for good citizenship in a free society. And it is certainly reasonable to examine other aspects of the schools and the school district that might bear on this question of *all*. For example, citizens will quite reasonably want to look at matters of educator expectations of student learning: do educators hold the same high expectations for all, or do some educators expect little (and thus will likely get little) from low-income students? Or, for example, are members of some ethnic groups disciplined far more often and more severely than members of other groups?

There is virtually no aspect of civic education program development and improvement that does not have some implications for virtually every other aspect of overall school and school district operation. All is (or should be, or can be made to be) open for thoughtful inspection and consideration. There might well be an advantage in eschewing what might be seen as a direct and overly critical attack on the overall system—an approach that might simply create defensive pushback—in favor of focusing on civic education, with examination of the overall system an almost incidental but now seen as necessary task.

A second consequence of the civic education program effort is that when you take on these tasks, and particularly when you take on these tasks in concert with others, you are helping yourself and others to enact and re-enact what it means to be a citizen in a free society. In working on civic education (and consequently working on overall issues of potential disparity), you are affirming a free society. Your commitment to bequeathing something of value and trying to make sure generations to come value what you are bequeathing is an affirmation. Affirming is a critical part of sustaining.

A third consequence of the civic education program effort is the development of greater thoughtfulness through deeper understanding. The problems we are dealing with are difficult problems. Were these problems amenable to quick and effective solutions, the problems would have been taken care of decades ago. As we work together, we are more likely to realize that it is unreasonable to expect quick solutions. And with that understanding, we will have more reasonable expectations. It does no good for any of us, whatever kind of stakeholders we might be, to condemn educators as ineffectual because they have not caused significant drops in test score discrepancies within a year or two. We of course want to maintain high expectations—of others and of ourselves. But to "darkeneth counsel by words without knowledge" (Job 38:2) and by irresponsible expectations is pointless and unproductive.

A fourth consequence of the civic education program effort is the development of social capital, trust, and skills in working better together. Citizens and educators who come together in this one effort can find that sometime later the next task—say, consideration of rebuilding or building anew a high school structure—is taken on and accomplished with a bit more ease. And so, too, the task after that. Trust begets trust, and if care is taken to fold newcomers to the school district into the development and involvement process, that trust can be extended. It is sometimes said that insanity is doing the same thing over and over and expecting different results. More properly, we might say that if you do the same thing more or less over and over again, while making slight corrective adjustments in response to feedback (learning), you can get better results.

John Adams famously observed that he "must study Politicks and War that my sons may have liberty to study Mathematicks and Philosophy. My sons ought to study Mathematicks and Philosophy, Geography, natural History, Naval Architecture, navigation, Commerce and Agriculture, in order to give their Children a right to study Painting, Poetry, Musick, Architecture, Statuary, Tapestry, and Porcelaine."[29] A careful optimism, what with "ought to study" and a "right to study," but progression nonetheless.

But when we consider our reliance on schools as the place for passing along the skills and values of a free society, we see little chance of steady progress. The schools are imperfect although amenable to improvement. They are equally capable of supporting equality and inequality. They remain our best but practically only choice in looking to sustain a free society. In seeking to use and improve schools, our task is Sisyphean. There are always new sets of students, new sets of families, new staff, and new community members. There is little that we can put in place that cannot and probably will not be interpreted differently or just plain ignored by those following.

What we do for the next generation must in turn be done again by the next generation for theirs following and in turn done again. Aiming for a recognition of perennial value, we do the best we can.

NOTES

1. Alexis de Tocqueville, *Democracy in America*, trans. Harvey C. Mansfield and Delba Winthrop (Chicago: University of Chicago Press, 2000), 171–72.

2. *New York Sun*, as quoted in Richard Hofstadter, *Anti-Intellectualism in American Life* (New York: Knopf, 1964), 303.

3. For recent data on schooling, see Maya Riser-Kositsky, "Education Statistics: Facts about American Schools," *Education Week*, January 3, 2019 (updated June 16, 2020), https://www.edweek.org/leadership/education-statistics-facts-about-american-schools/2019/01.

4. Roger Soder, "When I Get My Own Classroom," in *The Teaching Career*, eds. John I. Goodlad and Timothy J. McMannon (New York: Teachers College Press, 2004).

5. On school districts in Washington State, see Washington State Board of Education, "Report and Recommendations to the 1957 Legislature: School District Organization under Chapter 395, Laws of 1955, School District Organization Act,"

January 1957, https://babel.hathitrust.org/cgi/pt?id=uiug.30112088250581&view=1up&seq=8.

6. Daniel Arkin, "College Cheating Scandal: Why Some American Families Go after Elite Schools," *NBC News*, March 21, 2019, https://www.nbcnews.com/news/us-news/college-cheating-scandal-why-some-american-families-go-after-elite-n985576.

7. There is a considerable literature on school-society correspondence. One classic in the field is Samuel Bowles and Herbert Gintis, *Schooling in Capitalist America: Educational Reform and the Contradictions of Economic Life* (New York: Basic Books, 1976).

8. Tocqueville, *Democracy in America*, 325. See also Claudio Saunt, *Unworthy Republic: The Dispossession of Native Americans and the Road to Indian Territory* (New York: Norton, 2020).

9. Tocqueville, *Democracy in America*, 346.

10. For a useful perspective, see Edward E. Baptist, *The Half That Has Never Been Told: Slavery and the Making of American Capitalism* (New York: Basic Books, 2014).

11. See Douglas A. Blackmon, *Slavery by Another Name: The Re-Enslavement of Black Americans from the Civil War to World War II* (New York: Doubleday, 2008).

12. Kriston McIntosh, Emily Moss, Ryan Nunn, and Jay Shambaugh, "Examining the Black–White Wealth Gap," Brookings Institution, February 27, 2020, https://www.brookings.edu/blog/up-front/2020/02/27/examining-the-black-white-wealth-gap/.

13. Sarah Hansen, "Here's What the Racial Wealth Gap in America Looks Like Today," *Forbes*, June 5, 2020, https://www.forbes.com/sites/sarahhansen/2020/06/05/heres-what-the-racial-wealth-gap-in-america-looks-like-today/?sh=33a22769164c. See also Moritz Kuhn, Moritz Schularick, and Ulrike I. Steins, "Income and Wealth Inequality in America, 1949–2016," *Journal of Political Economy* 128, no. 2 (September 2020): 3469–3519.

14. For the National Urban League's *State of Black America* reports, see https://soba.iamempowered.com.

15. Jaclyn Diaz, "Air Force Investigation Finds Black Members Face Racial Disparity in Service," *NPR*, December 22, 2020, https://www.npr.org/2020/12/22/949082798/air-force-investigation-finds-black-members-face-racial-disparity-in-service.

16. Rebecca Morin, "Percentage Grows among Americans Who Say Black People Experience a 'Great Deal' of Discrimination, Survey Shows," *USA Today*, June 8, 2020, https://www.usatoday.com/story/news/politics/2020/06/08/survey-higher-percentage-us-agree-black-people-face-discrimination/3143651001/. See also Monica Anderson, "For Black Americans, Experiences of Racial Discrimination Vary by Education Level, Gender," Pew Research Center, May 2, 2019, https://www.pewresearch.org/fact-tank/2019/05/02/for-black-americans-experiences-of-racial-discrimination-vary-by-education-level-gender/.

17. Again, the literature is vast. A useful way to gain access is through John Higham, *Strangers in the Land: Patterns of American Nativism 1860–1925* (New York: Atheneum, 1981).

18. National School Boards Association, https://www.nsba.org/Advocacy/Equity.

19. National PTA, https://www.pta.org/docs/default-source/default-document-library/dei-brief-final-072720.pdf.

20. Jill Barshay, "Inside the Reardon-Hanushek Clash over 50 Years of Achievement Gaps," *The Hechinger Report*, May 27, 2019, https://hechingerreport.org/inside-the-reardon-hanushek-clash-over-50-years-of-achievement-gaps/.

21. For a comprehensive summary and analysis, see Robert D. Putnam, *Our Kids: The American Dream in Crisis* (New York: Simon & Schuster, 2015).

22. George Counts, *The Selective Character of Secondary Education* (Chicago: University of Chicago Press, 1922), 156.

23.[#]"Shutting Schools Has Hit Poor American Children's Learning," *The Economist* December 19, 2020, https://www.economist.com/united-states/2020/12/19/shutting-schools-has-hit-poor-american-childrens-learning.

24. For an earlier sense of civic education curriculum concerns, see Lorraine Smith Pangle and Thomas L. Pangle, *The Learning of Liberty: The Educational Ideas of the American Founders* (Lawrence: University Press of Kansas, 1993).

25. For a description of how such coffee hours worked in one school district, see James R. Lowham and William Mester as Told to Barbara A. Lippke and Eugene B. Edgar, "A Tale of Two Districts," in *Education and the Making of a Democratic People*, eds. John I. Goodlad, Roger Soder, and Bonnie McDaniel (Boulder, Colo.: Paradigm, 2008), 154.

26. Raymond Aron, *Main Currents in Sociological Thought*, trans. Richard Howard and Helen Weaver (New York: Doubleday, 1968), 274.

27. For discussion of some of the complexities of measuring civic education learning, see Roger Soder, "The Double Bind of Civic Education Assessment and Accountability" in *Holding Accountability Accountable: What Ought to Matter in Public Education*, ed. Kenneth A. Sirotnik (New York: Teachers College Press, 2004).

28. The notion of close connections between teacher education and the K-12 schools is usefully developed in John I. Goodlad's *Teachers for Our Nation's Schools* (San Francisco: Jossey-Bass, 1990) and his *Educational Renewal: Better Teachers, Better Schools* (San Francisco: Jossey-Bass, 1994). In 1986, Goodlad and colleagues created the National Network for Educational Renewal, a collection of school-university partnerships focusing on the simultaneous renewal of teacher education programs and the schools. For information regarding ongoing work of the National Network for Educational Renewal, see https://nnerpartnerships.org/?doing_wp_cron=1610659022.8033289909362792968750.

29. "John Adams to Abigail Adams, 12 May 1780," Founders Online, National Archives, https://founders.archives.gov/documents/Adams/04-03-02-0256.

Chapter 6

The Free Society: Reflections and Directions

If we meet the conditions we have postulated for a free society, and if leaders, citizens, and schools fulfill the roles we have specified, can we be assured of a free society? The answer is a qualified "yes." We will be able to enjoy and perhaps abuse some of the rudiments of a free society, and we will be able to preserve at least for some time the institutions and procedures—if not the habits of mind—of a free society.

But if we want to move from a qualified "yes" to one more solid, then we must deal with three elements that are critical in determining the durability—and even more important, the quality—of a free society. Those elements are (1) the extent to which citizens behave in ways so that they *deserve* a free society, (2) the extent to which citizens can and do entertain notions of *possibility* as well as probability, and (3) the extent to which citizens embrace their moral obligation to *pay attention* to other people.

DESERVING A FREE SOCIETY

In several parts of his *Revolutions Revisited*, Ralph Lerner is careful to stress the notion of deserving. He speaks of "behaving like a people who deserved a free society" and "the hatred that free individuals (or those who deserve to be free) harbor for absolute power." Elsewhere, we find "a studied effort to win and deserve," as well as "their manner of speaking invites a people to assent, and to deserve to assent, a sense of national pride."[1] When a very careful writer repeatedly makes such distinctions, we are bound to examine with equal care.

Lerner is not alone in his concern for what "deserve" might mean for citizens in a free society. In England during World War II, a popular poster showed Winston Churchill, or rather a part of him—face, bow tie, hand pointing out at the viewer—and underneath him, just two words: "Deserve Victory." Not, "get victory." Not "make victory yours" or "be victorious." The poster is a reminder that "deserve" must be considered as part of a response to Churchill's own question, "What kind of people do they think we are?" John Adams, too, had some sense of the matter: in a letter to Abigail, he observes that "We cannot insure Success, but We can deserve it."[2]

There are many ways to approach the notion of being deserving. In our everyday going about the world, we speak of getting your just deserts. The lawbreaker got (or didn't get) what he deserved. Or, we sometimes say, after a bad day where nothing seemed to go well, "I didn't deserve this." We speak of making our bed and then lying in it. We think, too, of reaping what you sow or, beyond that, sowing the wind and reaping the whirlwind.

"Deserve" is a salient feature of sports events. After a close game, some fans on the losing side will be heard to say that their team actually deserved the victory, and the only reason the other team supposedly won was because of luck or biased calls by officials. Such complaints and excuses are sometimes similarly heard after election day.

In the formal realm of moral philosophy, of ethics, the notion of "deserve" and its many counterparts is treated at length and with considerable complexity.[3] The notion of deserving, of desert, is connected to notions of distributive justice and ways to adjudicate distribution of scarce resources. Desert is also linked to ways of framing questions of fairness and equity and equality. And there are distinctions to be made between deserve, merit, and entitlement.

For our purposes here, a more modest approach is in order. We will focus on behavior (in the sense of Lerner's "behave like a people who deserved a free society"), not on theory, and specifically on behavior as citizens in a free society.

To deserve a free society, we have to *work* at it, we have to act on the basis of our responsibilities to secure and sustain that society. As such, we cannot deserve a free society if we think we should have a free society just because we are of a certain social or economic class or belong to a certain group. And we cannot deserve a free society if we are ignorant of our responsibilities or—perhaps even more problematic—we have some knowledge of our responsibilities but can't be bothered because we are too busy getting and spending.

The behaviors necessary to deserve a free society are those we have been speaking of throughout this volume. Taking part in the social and political process. Helping to identify and support good leaders. Being knowledgeable of the past as well as the present. Insisting that we become and stay a more thoughtful public. Insisting on clear language and recognition of facts. Working with schools, working with neighborhood community groups. Knowing and acting on the difference between self-interest and Tocqueville's "self-interest well understood." These are behaviors, behaviors stemming from good habits of mind. If we exhibit such behaviors, we stand a reasonable chance of securing and sustaining a free society because we know what is at stake.

If we do not behave in ways to deserve a free society, we might very well lose what we have. As Ralph Lerner reminds us, "In the last analysis, what matters is the character of the people. Those who prize liberty only instrumentally for the externals it brings—ease, comfort, riches—are not destined to keep it long."[4] Moreover, if by chance we have a free society at least for a while, there will be long odds of being able to bequeath it because people will have little understanding of just what there is to bequeath.

Consider what some of us do in thinking about possessions that might be left to family and friends. Think of photos, books, an old fountain pen, all sorts of prized possessions that we either obtained directly or were passed down to us from those who came before. We sometimes tell children and others the back story, the details of how something that looks old and shabby and not worth bothering with actually has great meaning to you, and thus—you hope—will have great meaning to them later on. We let them know the reason why something is worth keeping. What we do with possessions we pass along, we surely need to do when trying to ensure that future generations will know the real meaning—the true value—of a free society so they in turn can keep it and bequeath it.

We need to note that not everyone will be able to act equally on their obligations as citizens. For those with means, it is not difficult to find time to serve on committees, volunteer at a child's school, or otherwise behave in ways making one deserving of a free society. There are many others who do not have that kind of discretionary time. They are struggling at two low-paying jobs separated by long commutes, just trying to keep afloat.

Even so, despite all of the time pressures, citizens can find opportunities to talk with their children or neighbors about civic matters and the importance of knowing what is going on, what the issues are, and how to work through policy trade-offs. Children are remarkably quick at picking up what adults value as important, and it does not take long disquisitions for them to learn about their role in a free society.

Not everyone in a free society, rich or poor, behaves in ways to deserve that society, yet they enjoy that society's benefits.[5] They are in this respect free riders, getting the benefits without contributing to the costs. How might we view them? We don't want to say to them "you are behaving inappropriately and we're banishing you to the wilderness to live in solitude and shame." And we don't say to those who are only partially behaving inappropriately that they can stay but will be denied certain benefits.

There are two reasons why we don't treat free riders in this way. First, the actual argument for deserving a free society is usually vague in many respects. To reduce that vagueness, we would need an argument as follows: To deserve a free society (with free society defined precisely as A) people have to exhibit X behaviors as indicated by adherence (as measured by Y) to a set of standards (specified as Z). Such an argument is difficult to make. How, for example, can we talk in precise and legal terms about someone's unwillingness to act on reasonable understanding of the difference between self-interest and self-interest well understood? It would be unethical and illegal to deny benefits when vagueness is so predominant.

The second reason for not banishing free riders or otherwise denying them benefits is that we do not want to limit the opportunities to help free riders come to a better understanding of their obligations. As it happens, the notion of limiting one's chances of measuring up because you don't measure up is a common response. A child not doing well is school is suspended from school, thus exacerbating the problem: how can you have the opportunity to do better in school when you're not allowed to attend school?

The only practical response to the free rider problem in a free society is to recognize that those whose behavior suggests they do not deserve a free society are likely not going to change in response to our major concerted efforts. We can at most hope for change coming as a result of low-key strategies, and as free riders change in small ways here and there, we can build on those changes and hope for more.

THE POSSIBILITY OF POSSIBILITIES

When considering the need to think in terms of possibilities, Ralph Lerner again gives us much to work with. Lerner suggests that true statesmen such as Burke, Lincoln, and Tocqueville "see fit to make arguments that point beyond the accidental and contingent, beyond the transient issues of the day. They direct the attention of their contemporaries and successors to human possibilities that any and every people might hold in regard and strive for."[6]

What is possible is related to what is probable. But there are significant differences. Economist Albert Hirschman makes the distinction between the two as follows:

> Most social scientists conceive it as their exclusive task to discover and stress regularities, stable relationships, and uniform sequences. This is obviously an essential search, one in which no thinking person can refrain from participating. But in the social sciences there is a special room for the opposite type of endeavor: to underline the multiplicity and creative disorder of the human

adventure, to bring out the uniqueness of a certain occurrence, and to perceive an entirely new way of turning a historical corner.

Beyond that, Hirschman tells us, we need to consider "an approach to the social world that would stress the unique rather than the general, the unexpected rather than the expected, and the possible rather than the probable. . . . to widen the limits of what is or is perceived to be possible, be it at the cost of lowering our ability . . . to discern the probable."[7]

To speak of the possible smacks of impracticality, of Shakespeare's 107th sonnet, "the prophetic soul of the wide world, dreaming on things to come." We tend to dismiss talk of what might be possible in favor of what we know. We are, as we have noted throughout this volume, often in a hurry, and we act on the basis of what we know (or think we know), a calculation of the odds of the immediately probable.

The search for the probable, as Hirschman says, is something no thinking person will deny. There are, after all, pressures of time and lack of resources. To take the time and resources to analyze not only the immediately identifiable probable but also all of the possible options is very often indefensible. Engineers determining bridge specifications take into consideration probable stress from wind, storm, and earthquake, but only to the extent limited by the probability of what might happen in the next hundred years. A thousand-year storm generated by a meteor hitting Earth will not factor into the calculations, and all of us, engineers and non-engineers alike, will understand.

But in the realm of politics, there are often circumstances in which the possible is peremptorily denied a hearing. Thus, a newly elected legislator speaks of putting forth a bill to revamp a state's antiquated and ill-working tax structure. Veteran legislators will immediately chime in with, "Don't bother. There is zero chance of tax structure reform ever passing." And thus a new member of the school board speaks of a possibility of rejecting all of the state's requirements for standardized testing only to be told very quickly by other board members that the public would never stand for such a move.

We need the possible, we need to dream, to think, to go beyond trimming our sails to meet our calculated probabilities. There is more out there than is dreamt of in our philosophy. Educational philosopher Maxine Greene quotes colleague Mary Warnock: "There are vast unexplored areas, huge spaces of which we may get only an occasional awe-inspiring glimpse, questions raised by experience about whose answers we can only with hesitation experience."

We need to be open, Greene says, to the "unexplored." And it is through imagination that we can open windows "in the actual and the taken-for-granted toward what might be and what is not yet."[8]

Imagination, then, opens us up to possibilities beyond probabilities. But imagination does much more. "Imagination," historian James Axtell says, "is the key to moral understanding. Lack of it blinds us as seriously as it did the European colonialists who savagely killed Indians and enslaved Africans." Axtell goes on to remind us of Margaret Atwood's observation that "Oppression involves a failure of the imagination: the failure to imagine the full humanity of other human beings."[9]

Imagination allows us to empathize. We can at least get a glimpse of what is going on with others, what their needs are. It is only a glimpse, however, given that we are never quite sure. For example, some years back, I received from a student a summary of a report of a mission trip to a poor village in some part of the third world. The report ended with a cautionary and laudatory note that, although the visitors left feeling they had done a great deal of good, there was no way of knowing just what the villagers thought.

Imagining possibilities, dreaming on things to come, has limits that must be respected. We can remind ourselves of the cautionary tale of Icarus who disregards limits and flies too close to the sun with the inevitable result. And we can think of Faust, filled with visions of imagined possibilities, making a daring and ultimately self-defeating wager with the Devil: if you can ever satisfy me, you can have my soul. Overreaching and never being satisfied, always thinking of yet other possibilities, are reflected, too, in the observation of imperialist and scholarship founder Cecil Rhodes: "I would annex the planets if I could. I think of that often. It makes me sad to see them so clear and yet so far."[10]

We have to consider, then, that imagination, for all of its many advantages and great potential, is not enough and in fact can be dangerous left on its own. Imagination must be coupled with a disciplined sense of the probable, the notion of what is likely to happen in this world, both the physical world and the social world. A disciplined sense implies some kind of rigor. Imagination must be joined with rigor, as Gregory Bateson stresses. He speaks of the two as the "great contraries of mental process, either of which by itself is lethal. Rigor alone is paralytic death, but imagination alone is insanity."[11]

It is that kind of imagination coupled with rigor, that notion of possibilities, that ability to "widen the limits of what is or is perceived to be possible" that we in a free society must value and encourage. If we simply stick with the probable, we will probably get by. The institutions and procedures and societal structures will likely be around for a while if only because of inertia and our not paying heed. But to become more, to be able to respond to the unknown, and to contemplate what we might yet strive for in a free society, we need high regard for the possibility of possibilities.

Within the limits we have noted, opening ourselves to possibilities beyond the probable is a potential good in terms of a free society. We are faced with many complex challenges in the world—climate change is but one such challenge—and if we are to survive at all, let alone survive as citizens in a free society, we need to move beyond uncritical and casual acceptance of assumptions and the usual range of approaches. We are going to need all the help we can get, and much of that help can come from being willing to seek out and listen to perhaps odd possibilities combined in new ways.

But we need to go beyond considering possibilities as a means, and consider possibilities as ends in themselves, just as we need to consider and value all people as ends, not means. In this, we can entertain possibilities, in the words of organizational theorist James March, as helping us become "interesting people, interesting organizations, and interesting societies in the world."[12]

THE MORAL OBLIGATION TO PAY ATTENTION TO OTHER PEOPLE

In adverting to the moral obligation to pay attention to other people, it may seem that we are simply revisiting and reframing Tocqueville's notion of "self-interest well understood." Of course, we may say, it is clear that I cannot simply look out for myself while ignoring others: others can have a negative impact on me or on the larger group so I'm on the alert. (Or, as a colleague once said, "I vote for school levies because although I don't have children in school I have to live with yours.")

But there is much more to weigh and consider. Paying attention to others as self-interest well understood puts the emphasis on a functionalist perspective. We typically frame this approach as a question: How does paying attention to others function as part of the way to keep a free society operating over time? We can try to answer our own question, but when the question is framed in a functionalist way, we run the risk of limiting ourselves to a functionalist response.

Another way of framing lands us elsewhere—and let us hope a better elsewhere. We can ask ourselves: Regardless of what may or may not go on in a free society, do we have a moral obligation to pay attention to other people? And what are the costs when we don't pay attention?

There are three sources from the world of fiction that we can draw on in considering these questions.

The first source is Dostoevsky's *Notes from Underground*, a monologue in which we hear from a clerk in the Russian bureaucracy, a clerk who sees himself as "sick," as "wicked," as "unattractive." He is, above all, resentful, and his resentment in part stems from the way nobody pays attention to him. Our clerk tells us of a central experience, his encounter with a military officer in "some wretched little tavern." "I was standing beside the billiard table, blocking the way unwittingly, and he wanted to pass; he took me by the shoulders and silently—with no warning or explanation—moved me from where I stood to another place, and then passed by as if without noticing. I could even have forgiven a beating, but I simply could not forgive his moving me and in the end just not noticing me."[13]

Our clerk spends years dreaming of getting even, of plotting to get back at the officer. His plan is to meet the officer on the busy sidewalk and deliberately refuse to step aside. After many unsuccessful attempts, at long last, he contrives to bump into the officer "by accident" and does not give way. The officer does not even look back, although our clerk is somehow convinced that the officer noticed him.

From a functionalist standpoint, the resentment the clerk feels does not make any sort of positive contribution to a free society. All those years of planning to take revenge, to get even, to at the very least get noticed, from a societal perspective, could have better been spent on volunteer work, on serving on neighborhood planning committees, or tutoring the young in schools. And from an immediately practical standpoint, some might say our clerk is greatly overreacting and needs to just forget what he thinks happened to him.

But we need to move beyond viewing the clerk's behavior in terms of benefit or disadvantage to a free society. The point is that the clerk feels bad, feels less of a human being, because he is not being noticed. The officer in the tavern makes no distinction between a human being and a piece of furniture. No matter the effect on society, the clerk should not have been treated that way. And whether we feel that the clerk is overreacting or not, the point is that the *clerk* feels bad, and he surely is not going to feel less bad and less resentful just because we tell him to just get over it. Our abrupt dismissal of the clerk's pain might provoke even more resentment because of our evident unwillingness to really listen to what the clerk is trying to say.

Our second source is Horatio Alger's 1867 *Ragged Dick*, the first of many dozens of young adult "strive and succeed" morality novels. The novels—some 20 million copies sold by the 1920s—were formulaic and superficial, with little psychological insight. An honest lad overcomes poverty and nasty villains by a combination of a bit of luck and a good deal of hard work. As the progenitor, *Ragged Dick* initiates the formula, but unlike those that follow, it sometimes moves to curiously brief but deeper ground. That deeper ground is worth more than a glance.

Dick, a shoeshine boy, lives on the streets of New York. One day he is asked by a wealthy man to look after the man's nephew for the day, show him the sights, while the man is engaged in business. Off they go, returning to the uncle's house at the end of the day. Frank, the nephew, expresses his gratitude for the day by giving a set of his extra clothes to Dick. Frank, brings forth a suit, a shirt, a pair of shoes. One item he doesn't have: "I'm sorry I haven't any cap," he says.

"I've got one," said Dick.

"It isn't so new as it might be," said Frank, surveying an old felt hat, which had once been black, but was now dingy, with a large hole in the top and a portion of the rim torn off.

"No," said Dick; "my grandfather used to wear it when he was a boy, and I've kep' it ever since out of respect for his memory. But I'll get a new one now."

And so he does:

> Dick succeeded in getting quite a neat-looking cap, which corresponded much better with his appearance than the one he had on. The last, not being considered worth keeping, Dick dropped on the sidewalk, from which, on looking back, he saw it picked up by a brother boot-black who appeared to consider it better than his own.[14]

What are we to make of Ragged Dick? We know that by the end of the sequel to the novel that he has become upwardly mobile, known as Richard Hunter, Esquire, engaged to the daughter of a wealthy businessman. It would seem that other people are paying attention to him, noticing him. But when we read of Dick and his grandfather's cap, we realize that Dick isn't paying attention to himself or to his grandfather.

Paying attention over time is hard to do. Even best intentions can be knocked akilter by external events. Here is Dick, continuing to wear an old cap, a cap his grandfather wore when *he* was a boy. The cap is old, we know from the careful detailed description. And we have a sense of just how old by calculating the time from the grandfather's youth to Dick's current age. And readers of the entire novel will know that Dick is an orphan and that no other family member is to be seen. The only connection in the past that Dick can pay attention to is that sad battered cap.

That attention, respect for the grandfather's memory, is paid for many years. But just like that, attention is gone. A suit of clothes appears out of nowhere, and that old cap is suddenly out of place. It doesn't fit the classier look of our now up-and-coming Richard Hunter, Esquire. The rapidity of change is striking. Dick has just uttered words of attention and respect about his grandfather, only to turn, seconds later, to getting a new cap. He doesn't even think about the possibility of at least keeping his grandfather's cap in his shoeshine box (it surely wouldn't take much room). He throws his grandfather's cap on the sidewalk. It is only with what might be some fleeting regret he looks back for a moment to see the last of his only connection to the past.

Perhaps Dick feels fine and will continue to feel fine in his new role. Perhaps he has no regrets because he no longer knows what he had. But there might be costs in not paying attention, even if we don't acknowledge to ourselves that something we might actually need is missing.

In subsequent novels in the "strive and succeed" series, the strivers go about their business without regrets and without paying attention to other people, other than the attention paid to making sure success is in the offing. We can only speculate as to why Alger gave us this brief and sad insight in the first novel, only to not repeat. Alger certainly is no Dostoevsky. But for whatever reasons, Alger does push us to pay attention and to think about the costs to our own well-being in not paying attention.

Our third fictional source is R. F. Delderfield's novel, *To Serve Them All My Days*, a sympathetic account of life between the Great War and World War II at an English countryside boys public school. In its some six hundred pages, we find many insights worth pondering, one that is particularly noteworthy as we think about the obligation to pay attention. The event in question is a dinner honoring the retirement of Algernon Herries, headmaster, after many years of service. Following the usual speeches and presentations of gifts, the headmaster gives a short speech. The prose is distinctive. Rather than attempting to paraphrase, a few of the closing portions are quoted directly:

> "I've had plenty of first-class scholars through my hands since 1904, but I can't claim much credit for their academic successes. They would have been achieved at any school, given the same material. But helping to equip two generations of predatory males with the qualities of patience, tolerance, good fellowship and the ability to see someone else's point of view—qualities I see as the keystones of democracy—that's something else. . . . Let me close with a final anecdote, one that came to mind when I was riffling through the Old Boys' register this morning. . . .
>
> "It was a very trivial incident but it must have impressed me at the time. Why else should it have stayed in the mind for nearly twenty years? It concerned two boys, Petherick and 'Chuff' Rodgers, who accompanied me over to Barcombe by train. . . . It was Christmas time, of course, and the train was very full. We finally secured seats in a compartment where a young woman was nursing a baby. Within minutes of starting out the baby was dramatically sick . . . I remember poor Petherick's expression well, as he took refuge behind my copy of *The Times*. Upside down it was, but a thing like that wouldn't bother Petherick. He was one of our skyrockets, and went on to become president of a famous insurance company, and collect the O.B.E., or whatever they give the cream of insurance brokers. But I wasn't thinking so much of Petherick but of Chuff. Always unlucky, he had been sitting alongside the mother, and was thus on the receiving end of the business. I didn't know what to do but Chuff did. He whipped out a handkerchief—the only clean handkerchief I'd ever seen him sport—leaned across, wiped the baby's face and then the mother's lap. And when I say 'wiped' I mean wiped. It wasn't a dab. It was more of a general tidy-up, all round. After that we had a tolerably uneventful journey, with Rodgers making soothing noises all the way to the junction."

Headmaster Herries goes on to share why the incident is important to him:

> "It's very relevant, to me at any rate, relevant to what we've all been engaged in up here on the moor all these years. For Chuff Rodgers, bless his thick skull, never won a prize or a race in his life. Neither did he find time to do the only thing he was equipped to do—raise a family. He was killed at First Ypres, but I still remember him. Rather better than I remember Petherick. As a matter of fact, when I came across his name this morning, I thought of him as one of our outstanding successes."[15]

There might have been more to the headmaster's speech, the reader is told, but at this point there is prolonged applause from the audience, an emotional outpouring of great magnitude.

What emerges here? Some notions seem clear. The headmaster doesn't want to take much credit for the academic success of the school's students. Moreover, creating first-rate scholars is of less importance than attending to the keystones of democracy—those "qualities of patience, tolerance, good fellowship, and the ability to see someone else's point of view."

From here, the headmaster moves to the incident on the train and the very different responses of his two students, Petherick and Chuff. It is clear that there's not a lot of sympathy for Petherick. We are told Petherick is a success in the business world, possessor of the O.B.E. But that honor is quickly dismissed with "or whatever they give the cream of insurance brokers." When confronted with the results of the sick baby, Petherick ducks responsibility, hiding behind an upside down newspaper.

Chuff moves quickly, without calculation. He doesn't need to be told what to do (even though the headmaster apparently doesn't know how to respond). He acts in response to what he sees without a lot of fuss. He pays attention to the immediate needs. But, it is important to note, he follows up by making "soothing noises all the way to the junction." This followup is a critical matter. Chuff behaved decently enough with the cleanup and could have left it at that and gone about his business. But his attention and his concern extended beyond the immediate problem and instrumental response to a caring relationship with the baby and the mother.

We can see, then, three possible responses to the baby's behavior. Petherick's response of ignoring and hiding. The cleaning up of all concerned and then turning away. And Chuff's response: cleaning up and the following up, keeping alert and helping to make sure all is well. The first response clearly will not do. The second response is perhaps laudable, but it is limited, narrowly focused on solving the problem, not on relationships. It is this third response that can be linked to what is needed as one of the keystones for a democracy or, if you will, a free society—the need for ongoing relationships.

In the end, Chuff is killed in battle—the world is not fair—and Petherick becomes a success, reaching the presidency of a famous business and receiving the O.B.E. One might wonder if Petherick ever saw a uniform, let alone a battle, or whether he managed to dodge serving in the military as easily as he did the baby's sickness on the train.

Not all successful people act like our Petherick. There are many who are successful in their chosen work while reaching out and helping others through foundations, charities, and volunteer work. We can probably maintain a free society with the Pethericks doing what they do and not doing what they don't want to deal with. But it is not much of a society. The forms, the procedures, perhaps even some of the habits of mind can go on with the Pethericks of this world. But the quality of the free society might not be what it could be. With Chuff, a lot of Chuffs, we can speculate that the quality of life might be better, the society more decent.

But again, there's more to consider than the instrumental analysis of who and what contributes to a free society. In this short passage from the Delderfield novel, the headmaster appears to link qualities necessary for a democracy, with Chuff having those qualities and Petherick lacking them. But what matters is beyond instrumental consideration. What matters is that when we are on the train, we behave as Chuff and refuse to behave as Petherick.

Fiction, then, such as with Dostoevsky, Alger, and Delderfield, can provide us with insights into the moral obligation to pay attention. But beyond fiction, the everyday world is ours for the experiencing, and sometimes those experiences provide insights into what it means to pay attention to the world, and I close this volume with an account of two such experiences.

The first. I am riding on the bus from home to my university. The bus is a bit crowded, a few people standing, and no empty seats. I am sitting about six rows from the front. The bus stops, and an elderly woman with a cane comes on board. I see her, and I also see other riders in front of me across the aisle. Ahead of me on the other side is a young woman in the aisle seat. In front of her, also on the aisle, is a middle-aged man. I watch the man spot the elderly woman and then open his briefcase and take out a magazine. At the same time, I watch the young woman seated on the aisle behind him. She also sees the elderly woman. Just as the elderly woman finishes paying and is turning to see if a seat is available, the young woman has already gotten out of her seat. The elderly woman smiles, says thank you, sits down, and the young woman moves on further back. And off we go.

The second. Several summers ago, I was working in the yard, pruning this and that. After an hour, I took a break. Our house is some sixty feet from the street, with a concrete driveway coming up from the street to the house garage. I'm sitting on a wooden chopping block right by the house on the edge of the driveway. I'm resting and also leaning forward, staring down at cracks in the concrete that have been widening over the years. I'm thinking about the cost of patching versus a new driveway. And then I hear someone yelling, "Are you okay?" I look up. It's a neighbor, someone who lives further down our dead-end street. She's in her car, and the window is down. "I'm fine," I say. "Thanks for stopping." "Sure," she says, and drives on.

I was okay before she stopped. I was even better because she did.

I saw her again several days later. We talked some. I again thanked her for stopping, for paying attention. "No problem," she said. "I just wanted to be sure."

I hope that we—all of us—will always struggle to secure and sustain a free society. That is surely important. But more than that, I hope that we—all of us—can pay attention to others, stop, and be sure we're okay.

NOTES

1. Lerner, *Revolutions Revisited: Two Faces of the Politics of Enlightenment* (Chapel Hill: University of North Carolina Press, 1994), xii, 30, 44, 131.

2. "John Adams to Abigail Adams, 18 February 1776," *Founders Online*, National Archives, https://founders.archives.gov/documents/Adams/04-01-02-0229.

3. There are many useful summaries of philosophical approaches to the notion of deserving. See, for example, the entry on "Desert" in the *Stanford Encyclopedia of Philosophy.* https://plato.stanford.edu/entries/desert/. See also Serena Olsaretti, ed., *Desert and Justice* (New York: Oxford University Press, 2003).

4. Lerner, *Revolutions Revisited*, 127.

5. I offer my thanks to my former student, Alex Peterson, for useful conversations on these matters of deserving, not deserving, and free riders.

6. Lerner, *Revolutions Revisited*, 133.

7. A. O. Hirschman, *A Bias for Hope* (New Haven: Yale University Press, 1971), 27–28.

8. Maxine Greene, "Imagination and Learning: A Reply to Kiernan Egan," *Teachers College Record* 87, no. 2 (Winter 1985): 170. For Mary Warnock, see her *Imagination* (Berkeley: University of California Press, 1976), 207–8.

9. James Axtell, *Beyond 1492: Encounters in Colonial North America* (New York: Oxford University Press, 1992), 259. For Margaret Atwood, see *Second Words* (Toronto: Anansi, 1982), 397.

10. W. T. Stead, ed., *Last Will and Testament of Cecil John Rhodes* (London: "Review of Reviews" Office, 1902), 190.

11. Gregory Bateson, *Mind and Nature* (New York: Dutton, 1979), 219.

12. James March, "Model Bias in Social Action," *Review of Educational Research* 42 (Autumn 1972): 429.

13. Fyodor Dostoevsky, *Notes from Underground*, trans. Richard Pevear and Larissa Volokhonsky (New York: Vintage, 1993), 49.

14. Horatio Alger, *Ragged Dick and Mark, the Match Boy* (New York: Collier Books, 1962), 57–58, 65.

15. R. F. Delderfield, *To Serve Them All My Days* (New York: Simon & Schuster, 1972), 278–79.

Bibliography

Adams, John. "Adams' Argument for the Defense: 3-4 December 1770." *Founders Online*, National Archives. https://founders.archives.gov/documents/Adams/05-03-02-0001-0004-0016.

Adams, John. "Dissertation on the Canon and the Feudal Law." In *Papers of John Adams*, edited by Robert J. Taylor et al., vol. 1, no. 3. Cambridge, Mass.: Belknap Press, 1977.

Adams, John. "John Adams to Abigail Adams, 18 February 1776." *Founders Online*, National Archives. https://founders.archives.gov/documents/Adams/04-01-02-0229.

Adams, John. "John Adams to Abigail Adams, 12 May 1780." *Founders Online*, National Archives. https://founders.archives.gov/documents/Adams/04-03-02-0256.

Alger, Horatio. *Ragged Dick and Mark, the Match Boy*. New York: Collier Books, 1962.

Alterman, Eric. *When Presidents Lie: A History of Official Deception and Its Consequences*. New York: Viking, 2004.

American Prosperity Project. https://www.aspeninstitute.org/programs/business-and-society-program/american-prosperity-project/.

Anderson, Monica. "For Black Americans, Experiences of Racial Discrimination Vary by Education Level, Gender." Pew Research Center, May 2, 2019. https://pewresearch/org/fact-tank/2019/05/02/for-black-americans-experiences-of-racial-discrimination-vary-by-education-level-gender/.

Applebaum, Anne. *Twilight of Democracy: The Seductive Lure of Authoritarianism*. New York: Doubleday, 2020.

Arkin, Daniel. "College Cheating Scandal: Why Some American Families Go after Elite Schools." *NBC News*, March 21, 2019. http://www.nbcnews.com/news/us-news/college-cheating-scandal-why-some-american-families-go-after-elite-n985576.

Aron, Raymond. *Main Currents in Sociological Thought*. Translated by Richard Howard and Helen Weaver. New York: Doubleday, 1968.

Atwood, Margaret. *Second Word*s. Toronto: Anansi, 1982.

Axtell, James. *Beyond 1492: Encounters in Colonial North America*. New York: Oxford University Press, 1992.
Bacon, Francis. "Of Simulation and Dissimulation." In *Essays*, edited by John Pitcher. London: Penguin Books, 1985.
Baker, Peter. "Dishonesty Has Defined the Trump Presidency. The Consequences Could Be Lasting." *New York Times*, November 1, 2020.
Baptist, Edward E. *The Half That Has Never Been Told: Slavery and the Making of American Capitalism*. New York: Basic Books, 2014.
Barber, Bernard. *The Logic and Limits of Trust*. New Brunswick, N.J.: Rutgers University Press, 1983.
Barshay, Jill. "Inside the Reardon-Hanushek Clash over 50 Years of Achievement Gaps." *The Hechinger Report*, May 27, 2019. https://hechingerreport.org/inside-the-reardon-hanushek-clash-over-50-years-of-achievement-gaps/.
Barton, Dominic. "Capitalism for the Long Term." *Harvard Business Review* 89, no. 3 (March 2011): 84–91.
Barton, Dominic. "Refocusing Capitalism on the Long Term." *Oxford Review of Economic Policy* 33, no. 2 (Summer 2017): 188–210.
Bateson, Gregory. *Mind and Nature*. New York: Dutton, 1979.
Bateson, Gregory. *Steps to an Ecology of Mind*. New York: Ballantine, 1972; reissued with a foreword by Mary Catherine Bateson. Chicago: University of Chicago Press, 2000.
BBC News. "The Popularity of 'Time' Unveiled." June 22, 2006. news.bbc.co.uk/2/hi/uk_news/5104778stm.
Bellah, Robert N., Richard Madsen, William M. Sullivan, Ann Swidler, and Steven M. Tipton. *Habits of the Heart: Individualism and Commitment in American Life*. New York: Harper & Row, 1986.
Berry, Wendell. *Standing by Words*. San Francisco: North Point Press, 1983.
Blackmon, Douglas A. *Slavery by Another Name: The Re-Enslavement of Black Americans from the Civil War to World War II*. New York: Doubleday, 2008.
Blanda, Sean. "The Jeff Bezos School of Long-Term Thinking." March 2, 2013. https://www.seanblanda.com/the-jeff-bezos-school-of-long-term-thinking/.
Bok, Derek. *Higher Expectations: Can College Teach Students What They Need to Know for the Twenty-First Century?* Princeton: Princeton University Press, 2020.
Bowles, Samuel, and Herbert Gintis. *Schooling in Capitalist America: Educational Reform and the Contradictions of Economic Life*. New York: Basic Books, 1976.
Brand, Stewart. *The Clock of the Long Now: Time and Responsibility*. New York: Basic Books, 1999.
Brown, Patrick. "The Dark Side of Social Capital." *National Affairs* 40 (Summer 2019).
Brunner, Jim. "Loren Culp, Refusing to Concede Washington Gubernatorial Race, Turns on Top Republications," *Seattle Times*, November 21, 2020. https://www.seattletimes.com/seattle-news/politics/loren-culp-refusing to concede-washington-gubernatorial-race-turns-on-top-republicans.
Burke, Edmond. *Reflections on the Revolution in France*. Indianapolis: Bobbs-Merrill, 1957.

Camus, Albert. *The Plague*. Translated by Stuart Gilbert. New York: Knopf, 1980.
Carroll, Lewis. *Through the Looking Glass*. New York: Collier, 1962.
Chang, Jung. *Wild Swans: Three Daughters of China*. New York: Doubleday, 1991.
Chapman, Simon. "One Hundred and Fifty Ways the Nanny State is Good for Us." *The Conversation*, July 1, 2013. https://theconversation.com/one-hundred-and-fifty-ways-the-nanny-state-is-good-for-us-15587.
Chekhov, Anton. *Stories*. Translated by Richard Pevear and Larissa Volokhonsky. New York: Bantam, 2000.
Chisick, Harvey. *The Limits of Reform in the Enlightenment: Attitudes toward the Education of the Lower Classes in Eighteenth-Century France*. Princeton: Princeton University Press, 1981.
Churchill, Winston. "Their Finest Hour," Speech, London, June 18, 1940. International Churchill Society. https://winstonchurchill.org/resources/speeches/1940-the-finest-hour/their-finest-hour/.
Coleman, James. *Foundations of Social Theory*. Cambridge, Mass.: Belknap Press, 1990.
Conquest, Robert. *The Great Terror: A Reassessment*. New York: Oxford University Press, 1990.
Conquest, Robert. *The Harvest of Sorrow: Soviet Collectivization and the Terror-Famine*. New York: Oxford University Press, 1986.
Conquest, Robert. *Stalin: Breaker of Nations*. New York: Viking, 1991.
Cooley, Charles Horton. *Human Nature and the Social Order*. New York: Charles Scribner's Sons, 1902; New York: Taylor and Francis, 2017.
Counts, George. *The Selective Character of Secondary Education*. Chicago: University of Chicago Press, 1922.
Courtois, Stéphane, Nicolas Werth, Jean-Louis Panné, Andrzej Paczkowski, Karel Bartošek, and Jean-Louis Magolin. *The Black Book of Communism: Crimes, Terror, Repression*. Translated by Jonathan Murphy and Mark Kramer. Cambridge: Harvard University Press, 1999.
Dallek, Robert. *Flawed Giant: Lyndon Johnson and His Times, 1961-1973*. New York: Oxford University Press, 1998.
Delderfield, R. F. *To Serve Them All My Days*. New York: Simon & Schuster, 1972.
Dewey, John. "Creative Democracy—The Task before Us." In *John Dewey: The Later Works, 1925-1953, vol. 14, 1939–1941*. Edited by Jo Ann Boydston. Carbondale: Southern Illinois University Press, 1988.
Dewey, John. "Philosophies of Freedom." In *John Dewey: The Later Works, 1925-1953, vol. 3, 1927–1928*. Edited by Jo Ann Boydston. Carbondale: Southern Illinois University Press, 1984.
Diaz, Jaclyn. "Air Force Investigation Finds Black Members Face Racial Disparity in Service." *NPR*, December 22, 2020. https://www.npr.org/2020/12/22/949082798/air-force-investigation-finds-black-members-face-racial-disparity-in-service.
Dostoevsky, Fyodor. *The Brothers Karamazov*. Translated by Richard Pevear and Larissa Volkhonsky. San Francisco: North Point Press, 1990.
Dostoevsky, Fyodor. *Notes from Underground*. Translated by Richard Pevear and Larissa Volokhonsky. New York: Vintage, 1993.

Douglass, Frederick. "West India Emancipation," Speech, Canandaigua, New York, August 3, 1857. University of Rochester Frederick Douglass Project, https://rbscb.lib.rochester/4398.

Etzioni, Amitai. *The Active Society*. New York: Free Press, 1968.

Farr, James. "Social Capital." *Political Theory* 32, no. 1 (February 2004).

Faulkner, William. *Requiem for a Nun*. New York: New American Library, 1954.

FCLTGlobal. https://fcltglobal.org.

Fisher, Richard. "The Perils of Short-Termism: Civilization's Greatest Threat." *BBC*, January 9, 2019. https://www.bbc.com/future/article/20190109-the-perils-of-short-termism-civilisations-greatest-threat.

Flexner, Abraham. *Medical Education in the United States and Canada*. New York: Arno Press, 1972.

Fukuyama, Francis. *Identity: The Demand for Dignity and the Politics of Resentment.* New York: Farrar, Straus, and Giroux, 2018.

Fukuyama, Francis. *Trust: The Social Virtues and the Creation of Prosperity*. New York: Free Press, 1995.

Furnham, Adrian, and Joseph Marks. "Tolerance of Ambiguity: A Review of Recent Literature." *Psychology* 04 (September 2013): 717–28.

Georgia Public Policy Foundation. "The Atlanta Public Schools Cheating Scandal." https://www.georgiapolicy.org/issue/the-atlanta-public-schools-cheating-scandal/.

Gessner, Linda. "Knesset Commission for Future Generations." Foundation for Democracy & Sustainable Development, June 25, 2017. https://fdsd.org//?s=Knesset.

Gibbon, Edward. *The History of the Decline and Fall of the Roman Empire*. Vol. 2. Edited by David Womersley. London: Penguin Press, 1995.

Godio, Mili. "White House Press Secretary Kayleigh McEnany Wildly Exaggerates Trump March Crowd Size." *Newsweek*, November 14, 2020. https://www.newsweek.com/white-house-press-secretary-kayleigh-mcenany-wildly-exaggerates-trump-march-crowd-size-1547493.

Goodlad, John I. *Educational Renewal: Better Teachers, Better Schools*. San Francisco: Jossey-Bass, 1994.

Goodlad, John I. *Teachers for Our Nation's Schools*. San Francisco: Jossey-Bass, 1990.

Graham, John R., Campbell R. Harvey, and Shiva Rajgopal. "Value Destruction and Financial Reporting Decision." *Financial Analysts Journal* 62, no. 6 (Nov.-Dec. 2006): 27–39.

Greene, Maxine. "Imagination and Learning: A Repy to Kiernan Egan." *Teachers College Record* 87, no. 2 (Winter 1985): 167–71.

Hansen, Sarah. "Here's What the Racial Wealth Gap in America Looks Like Today." *Forbes*, June 5, 2020. https://www.forbes.com/sites/sarahhansen/2020/06/05/heres-what-the-racial-wealth-gap-in-america-looks-like-today/?sh=33a22769164c.

Hassan, Robert. *Empires of Speed: Time and the Acceleration of Politics and Society*. Boston: Brill, 2009.

Hastings, Max. *Winston's War: Churchill, 1940-1945*. New York: Knopf, 2010.

Haupt, William, III. "Op Ed: The 2020 Nanny State—The Good, the Bad and the Ugly." *The Center Square*, January 6, 2020. https://www.thecentersquare.com/national/op-ed-the-2020-nanny-state-the-good-the-bad-and-the-ugly/article_1031d970-308f-11ea-b471-174f6aadaa8a.html.

Herodotus. *The Persian Wars*. Translated by George Rawlinson. New York: Modern Library, 1942.

Higham, John. *Strangers in the Land: Patterns of American Nativism 1860-1925*. New York: Atheneum, 1981.

Hirschman, A. O. *A Bias for Hope*. New Haven: Yale University Press, 1971.

Hofstadter, Richard. *Anti-Intellecualism in American Life*. New York: Knopf, 1964.

Honoré, Carl. *In Praise of Slowness: Challenging the Culture of Speed*. San Francisco: HarperSanFrancisco, 2004.

Hughes, Langston. "Let America Be America Again." In *The Collected Poems of Langston Hughes* (New York: Knopf, 1994). https://poets.org/poem/let-america-be-america-again.

Ignatieff, Michael. *The Needs of Strangers: An Essay on Privacy, Solidarity, and the Politics of Being Human*. New York: Penguin, 1986.

Isaac, Mike, and Kellen Browning. "Fact-Checked on Facebook and Twitter," *New York Times*, November 11, 2020. https://www.nytimes.com/2020/11/1/technology/parler-rumble-newsmax.html?searchResultPosition=1.

Ishiguro, Kazuo. *The Remains of the Day*. New York: Vintage International, 1989.

Jefferson, Thomas. "Notes on Virginia." In *Writings*. New York: Library of America, 1984.

Jefferson, Thomas. "Revisal of the Laws, Bill no. 79, A Bill for the More General Diffusion of Knowledge," In *Writings*. New York: Library of America, 1984.

Kanter, Rosabeth Moss. *On the Frontiers of Management*. Cambridge: Harvard University Press, 1997.

Katz, Daniel, and Robert L. Kahn. *The Social Psychology of Organizations*. New York: Wiley, 1966.

Kelly, Kevin. "The Next 100 Years of Science: Long-Term Trends in the Scientific Method." The Long Now Foundation, Seminars about Long-Term Thinking, filmed March 10, 2006. http://longnow.org/seminars/02006/mar/10/long-term-trends-in-scientific method.

Krznaric, Roman. *The Good Ancestor: A Radical Prescription for Long-Term Thinking*. New York: The Experiment, 2020.

Krznaric, Roman. "Six Ways to Think Long-Term: A Cognitive Toolkit for Good Ancestors." Long Now Foundation, July 20, 2020. https://medium.com/the-long-now-foundation/six-ways-to-think-long-term-da373b3377a4.

Kuhn, Moritz, Moritz Schularick, and Ulrike I. Steins. "Income and Wealth Inequality in America, 1949–2016." *Journal of Political Economy* 128, no. 2 (September 2020): 3469–3519.

Kurland, Philip B., and Ralph Lerner, eds. *The Founders' Constitution*. Vol. 1. Chicago: University of Chicago Press, 1987.

Lasswell, Harold. *Politics: Who Gets What, When, How?* New York: McGraw-Hill, 1936.

Lerner, Ralph. *Maimonides' Empire of Light: Popular Enlightenment in an Age of Belief.* Chicago: University of Chicago Press, 2000.
Lerner, Ralph. *Revolutions Revisited: Two Faces of the Politics of Enlightenment.* Chapel Hill: University of North Carolina Press, 1994.
Lerner, Ralph. *The Thinking Revolutionary: Principle and Practice in the New Republic.* Ithaca: Cornell University Press, 1987.
Levitsky, Steven, and David Ziblatt. *How Democracies Die.* New York: Basic Books, 2018.
Lilla, Mark. *The Once and Future Liberal: After Identity Politics.* New York: Harper, 2017.
The Long Now Foundation. https://longnow.org.
Lowham, James R, and William Mester as Told to Barbara A. Lippke and Eugene B. Edgar. "A Tale of Two Districts." In *Education and the Making of a Democratic People,* edited by John I. Goodlad, Roger Soder, and Bonnie McDaniel, 139–160. Boulder, Colo.: Paradigm, 2008.
Madison, James. *Federalist* No. 51. In *The* Federalist, edited by Jacob E. Cooke. Middletown, Conn.: Wesleyan University Press, 1961.
March, James. "Model Bias in Social Action." *Review of Educational Research* 42 (Autumn 1972): 413–29.
March, James. "Yo sé quien soy." In *The Beat of a Different Drummer: Essays on Educational Renewal in Honor of John I. Goodlad,* edited by Kenneth A. Sirotnik and Roger Soder, 275–83. New York: Peter Lang, 1999.
Martin, Vince. "Short-Termism Isn't the Boogeyman You Think It Is." November 12, 2019. https://investorplace.com/2019/myth-short-termism-corporate-myopia-academic/.
McIntosh, Kriston, Emily Moss, Ryan Nunn, and Jay Shambaugh. "Examining the Black–White Wealth Gap." Brookings Institution, February 27, 2020. https://www.brookings.edu/blog/up-front/2020/02/27/examining-the-black-white-wealth-gap/.
Mead, George Herbert. *Mind, Self, & Society.* Edited by Charles W. Morris. 1934. Reprint, Chicago: University of Chicago Press, 1962.
Melton, James Van Horn. *Absolutism and the Eighteenth-Century Origins of Compulsory Schooling in Prussia and Austria.* Cambridge: Cambridge University Press, 1988.
Morin, Rebecca. "Percentage Grows among American Who Say Black People Experience a 'Great Deal' of Discrimination, Survey Shows." *USA Today,* June 8, 2020. https://www.usatoday.com/story/news/politics/2020/06/08/survey-higher-percentage-us-agree-black-people-face-discrimination/3143651001/.
Morozov, Evgeny. *The Net Delusion: The Dark Side of Internet Freedom.* New York: PublicAffairs, 2012.
Muller, Herbert J. *Freedom in the Western World: From the Dark Ages to the Rise of Democracy.* New York: Harper & Row, 1963.
Muller, Herbert J. *Issues of Freedom: Paradoxes and Promises.* New York: Harper & Brothers, 1960.
National Network for Educational Renewal. https://nnerpartnerships.org/?doing_wp_cron=1610659022.8033289909362792968750.

National PTA. https://www.pta.org/docs/default-source/default-document-library/dei-brief-final-072720.pdf.
National School Boards Association. https://www.nsba.org/Advocacy/Equity.
National Urban League. *State of Black America*. https://soba.iamempowered.com.
Nichols, Thomas M. *The Death of Expertise: The Campaign against Established Knowledge and Why It Matters*. New York: Oxford University Press, 2017.
Olsaretti, Serena, ed. *Desert and Justice*. New York: Oxford University Press, 2003.
Olson, Mancur. "Dictatorship, Democracy, and Development." *The American Political Science Review* 87, no. 3 (September 1993): 567–76.
Orwell, George. "Politics and the English Language." Vol. 4 of *The Collected Essays, Journalism and Letters of George Orwell*, edited by Sonia Orwell and Ian Angus. New York: Harcourt Brace Jovanovich, 1968.
Oxford Martin Commission for Future Generations. "Now for the Long Term: The Report of the Oxford Martin Commission for Future Generations." October 2013. https://www.oxfordmartin.ox.ac.uk/downloads/commission/Oxford_Martin_Now_for_the_Long_Term.pdf.
Pangle, Lorraine Smith, and Thomas L. Pangle. *The Learning of Liberty: The Educational Ideas of the American Founders*. Lawrence: University Press of Kansas, 1993.
Patrick, Stewart. "Looking Past the Inbox: Report of the Oxford Martin Commission for Future Generations." Council on Foreign Relations, November 6, 2013. https://www.cfr.org/blog/looking-past-inbox-report-oxford-martin-commission-future-generations.
Pembroke, Beatrice, and Ella Saltmarshe. "The Long Time." The Long Time Project, October 28, 2019. https://medium.com/@thelongtimeinquiry/the-long-time-3383b43d42ab.
Putnam, Robert D. *Bowling Alone*. New York: Simon & Schuster, 2000.
Putnam, Robert D. *Making Democracy Work: Civic Traditions of Modern Italy*. Princeton: Princeton University Press, 1993.
Putnam, Robert D. *Our Kids: The American Dream in Crisis*. New York: Simon & Schuster, 2015.
Putnam, Robert D. *The Upswing: How America Came Together a Century Ago and How We Can Do It Again*. New York: Simon & Schuster, 2020.
Rahe, Paul A. *Soft Despotism, Democracy's Drift: Montesquieu, Rousseau, Tocqueville, and the Modern Prospect*. New Haven: Yale University Press, 2009.
Revel, Jean-Francois. *How Democracies Perish*. New York: Doubleday, 1983.
Rifkin, Jeremy. *Time Wars: The Primary Conflict in Human History*. New York: Touchstone, 1989.
Riser-Kositsky, Maya. "Education Statistics: Facts about American Schools." *Education Week* January 3, 2019 (updated June 16, 2020). https://www.edweek.org/leadership/education-statistics-facts-about-american-schools/2019/01.
Rose, Jonathan. *The Intellectual Life of the British Working Classes*. New Haven: Yale University Press, 2001.

Rosenblum, Nancy L., and Russell Muirhead. *A Lot of People Are Saying: The New Conspiracism and the Assault on Democracy*. Princeton: Princeton University Press, 2020.

Runciman, David. *How Democracy Ends*. New York: Basic Books, 2018.

Saunt, Claudio. *Unworthy Republic: The Dispossession of Native Americans and the Road to Indian Territory*. New York: Norton, 2020.

Scheuerman, William E. *Liberal Democracy and the Social Acceleration of Time*. Baltimore: Johns Hopkins University Press, 2004.

Schulberg, Budd. *A Face in the Crowd*. New York: Ballantine, 1957.

Sebastian, Mikhail. *Journal 1935-1944: The Fascist Years*. Translated by Patrick Camiller. Chicago: Ivan Dee, 2000.

Semuels, Alana. "How to Stop Short-Term Thinking at America's Companies." *The Atlantic*, December 30, 2016. https://www.theatlantic.com/bus/archive/2016/12/short-term-thinking/511874.

"Shutting Schools Has Hit Poor American Children's Learning." *The Economist*, December 19, 2020. https://www.economist.com/united-states/2020/12/19/shutting-schools-has-hit-poor-american-childrens-learning.

Signer, Michael. *Demagogue: The Fight to Save Democracy from Its Worst Enemies*. New York: Palgrave Macmillan, 2009.

Smith, Adam. *The Theory of Moral Sentiments*. Vol. 1 of *The Glasgow Edition of the Works and Correspondence of Adam Smith*, edited by D. D. Raphael and A. L. Macfie. 1976. Reprint, Indianapolis: Liberty Fund, 1982.

Smith, Graham. "Why We Need a Committee for Future Generations in the House of Lords." June 5, 2018. https://constitution-unit.com/tag/oxford-martin-commission-for-future-generations/.

Snyder, Timothy. *On Tyranny: Twenty Lessons from the Twentieth Century*. New York: Tim Duggan Books, 2017.

Snyder, Timothy. *The Road to Unfreedom: Russia, Europe, America*. New York: Tim Duggan Books, 2018.

Soder, Roger. "The Double Bind of Civic Education Assessment and Accountability." In *Holding Accountability Accountable: What Ought to Matter in Public Education*, edited by Kenneth A. Sirotnik. New York: Teachers College Press, 2004.

Soder, Roger. "When I Get My Own Classroom." In *The Teaching Career*, edited by John I. Goodlad and Timothy J. McMannon. New York: Teachers College Press, 2004.

Stanford Encyclopedia of Philosophy. https://plato.stanford.edu/entries/desert/.

Stead, W. T., ed. *Last Will and Testament of Cecil John Rhodes*. London: "Review of Reviews" Office, 1902.

Stephen, Louise. "Obesity in Japan: Can the Metabo Law Prevent It?" February 24, 2018, https://louisestephen.com/2018/02/24/obesity-japan-can-metabo-law-prevent-it/.

Strauss, Leo. *Persecution and the Art of Writing*. Chicago: University of Chicago Press, 1952; 1988.

Thucydides. *The Peloponnesian War*. Translated by Richard Crawley. New York: Modern Library, 1951.

Tocqueville, Alexis de. *Democracy in America*. Translated by Harvey C. Mansfield and Delba Winthrop. Chicago: University of Chicago Press, 2000.

Tocqueville, Alexis de. "To Claude-François de Corcelle, September 17, 1853." In *Selected Letters on Politics and Society*, edited by Roger Boesche, translated by James Toupin and Roger Boesche. Berkeley: University of California Press, 1985.

Tocqueville, Alexis de. "To John Stuart Mill, March 18, 1841." In *Selected Letters on Politics and Society*, edited by Roger Boesche, translated by James Toupin and Roger Boesche. Berkeley: University of California Press, 1985.

Vevier, Charles, ed. *Flexner: 75 Years Later: A Current Commentary on Medical Education*. Lanham, Md.: University Press of America, 1987.

Wacjman, Judy. *Pressed for Time: The Acceleration of Time in Digital Capitalism*. Chicago: University of Chicago Press, 2015.

Walsh, Mary Roth. *Doctors Wanted: No Women Need Apply: Sexual Barriers in the Medical Profession, 1835-1975*. New Haven: Yale University Press, 1977.

Warnock, Mary. *Imagination*. Berkeley: University of California Press, 1976.

Washington State Board of Education. "Report and Recommendations to the 1957 Legislature: School District Organization under Chapter 395, Laws of 1955, School District Organization Act," January 1957. https://babel.hathitrust.org/cgi/pt?id=uiug.30112088250581&view=1up&seq=8.

Washington, George. *The Writings of George Washington*. Edited by J. C. Fitzpatrick. Vol. 30. Washington, D.C.: Government Printing Office, 1939.

Weaver, Richard. "Language is Sermonic." In *Language is Sermonic: Richard M. Weaver on the Nature of Rhetoric*. Edited by Richard L. Johannesen, Rennard Strickland, and Ralph T. Eubanks. Baton Rouge: Louisiana State University Press, 1970.

Weaver, Richard. "Reflections of Modernity." In *Life without Prejudice, and Other Essays*. Chicago: Regnery, 1965.

Whillans, Ashley. *Time Smart: How to Reclaim Your Time and Live a Happier Life*. Cambridge: Harvard Business Review Press, 2020.

White, James Boyd. "Heracles' Bow: Persuasion and Community in Sophocles' *Philoctetes*." In *Heracles' Bow: Essays on the Rhetoric and the Poetics of the Law*. Madison: University of Wisconsin Press, 1985.

White, James Boyd. *When Words Lose Their Meaning: Constitutions and Reconstitutions of Language, Character, and Community*. Chicago: University of Chicago Press, 1984.

Wittman, Marc. *Felt Time: The Science of How We Experience Time*. Translated by Eric Butler. Cambridge: MIT Press, 2017.

Wolin, Sheldon S. "What Time Is It?" *Theory and Event* 1, no. 1 (1997): 1–5.

Wordsworth, William. "The World is Too Much with Us." https://www.poetryfoundation.org/poems/45564/the-world-is-too-much-with-us.

Ziegler, Philip. *London at War 1939-1945*. New York: Knopf, 1995.

Zimbardo, Philip, and John Boyd. *The Time Paradox: The New Psychology of Time That Will Change Your Life*. New York: Free Press, 2008.

About the Author

Roger Soder is Professor Emeritus of Education at the University of Washington, Seattle. He joined with John Goodlad and Kenneth Sirotnik in creating the Center for Educational Renewal at the University of Washington (1985–2006). He was an officer of the related but independent Institute for Educational Inquiry (1992–2017). Prior to joining with Goodlad and Sirotnik in a deeply valued long-time collaboration, Soder was an administrator in the Cape Flattery School District on the Makah Indian Reservation at Neah Bay, Washington, and education director of the Seattle Urban League. Soder is the author of *The Language of Leadership* and editor of *Democracy, Education, and the Schools*. He is coeditor of *The Moral Dimensions of Teaching*, *Places Where Teachers Are Taught*, *Developing Democratic Character in the Young*, and *Education and the Making of a Democratic People*.

www.ingramcontent.com/pod-product-compliance
Lightning Source LLC
Chambersburg PA
CBHW021852300426
44115CB00005B/131